LANZAROTE

WINDRUSH · ISLAND GUIDES

LANZAROTE

John and Margaret Goulding

THE WINDRUSH PRESS
GLOUCESTERSHIRE

Acknowledgements
The authors would like to thank the Consejería de Turismo of the Cabildo Insular de Lanzarote (especially Enrique Alvarado, Miguel Ángel Martín and Esperanza Quevedo) for their prompt answers to a barrage of questions; also Araceli Rivera and Lydia Umpiérrez of the Tourist Information Offices in Arrecife and Puerto del Carmen. Thanks are also due to the Spanish National Tourist Office in London, to Ángel Sainz-Pardo of the Oficina Meteorológica del Aeropuerto de Lanzarote for help with the climate chapter, to Rosa María Armas de Lehmann for sharing her local knowledge, to Caroline Jebson and Gavin Longworth, to Dee Darters (once again), Club La Santa, INALSA and El Guincho.

A special thankyou to Larry Yaskiel of English *Lancelot*, who could not have been more helpful and supportive in supplying material for this third edition.

First published in Great Britain by
The Windrush Press,
Little Window,
High Street,
Moreton-in-Marsh,
Gloucestershire GL56 0YN
1989
Tel: 01608 652012   Fax: 01608 652125
Third revised and updated edition, 1997

Text and photographs © John and Margaret Goulding 1989, 1993, 1997

British Library Cataloguing in Publication Data
Goulding, John
  Lanzarote. – (Windrush island guide).
  1. Canary Islands. Gran Canaria, Lanzarote
  e Fuerteventura, – Visitor's guides
  I. Title   II. Goulding, Margaret
  916.4'9

  ISBN 0-900075-92-9

Typeset by DP Photosetting, Aylesbury, Bucks
Printed and bound in Hong Kong by Paramount Printing Group Ltd

Front cover illustration: Haría and Monte Corona from the Mirador de Haría
Back cover: cove at Papagayo

Dedicated to the Memory of

CÉSAR MANRIQUE (1919–1992)

CONTENTS

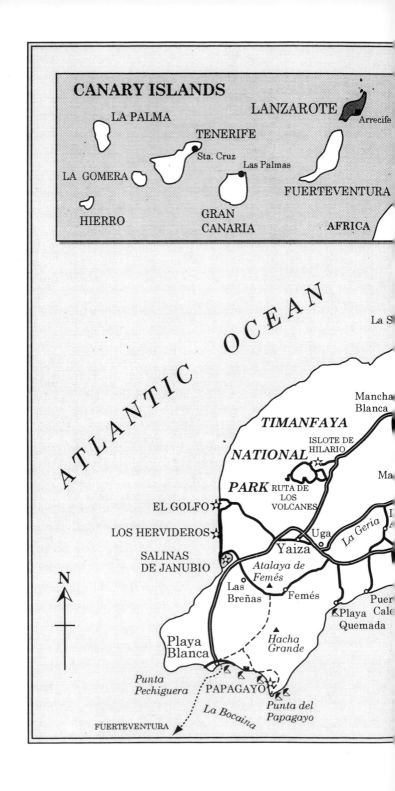

CANARY ISLANDS

LA PALMA

LANZAROTE

Arrecife

TENERIFE

Sta. Cruz

LA GOMERA

Las Palmas

HIERRO

GRAN
CANARIA

FUERTEVENTURA

AFRICA

OCEAN

La S

ATLANTIC

Mancha
Blanca

TIMANFAYA

ISLOTE DE
HILARIO

NATIONAL

Ma

PARK RUTA DE
LOS
VOLCANES

EL GOLFO ☆

LOS HERVIDEROS ☆

Uga

La Geria

I

SALINAS
DE JANUBIO ☆

Yaiza

Atalaya de
Femés

N

Las
Breñas

Femés

Puer
Cale

☆Playa
Quemada

Playa
Blanca

Hacha
Grande

Punta
Pechiguera

PAPAGAYO

Punta del
Papagayo

FUERTEVENTURA

La Bocaina

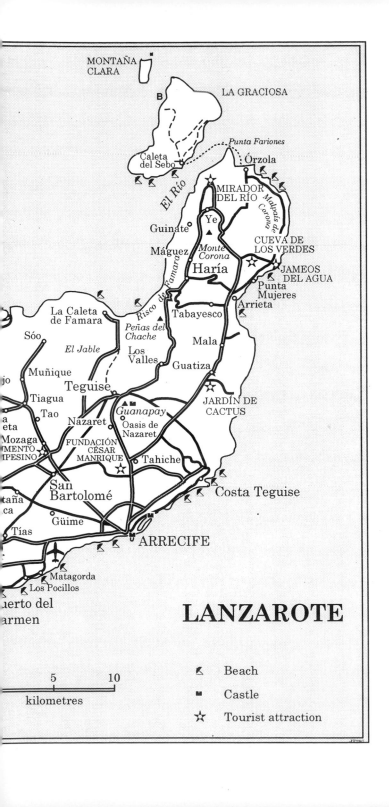

MONTAÑA
CLARA

LA GRACIOSA

B

Punta Fariones

Caleta
del Sebo

Órzola

El Río

MIRADOR
DEL RÍO

Malpaís de Corona

Guinate

Ye

*Monte
Corona*

Máguez

CUEVA DE
LOS VERDES

Haría

JAMEOS
DEL AGUA

Punta
Mujeres

Arrieta

Risco de Famara

La Caleta
de Famara

Tabayesco

Sóo

*Peñas del
Chache*

El Jable

Los
Valles

Mala

Muñique

Guatiza

Teguise

Tiagua

Guanapay

JARDÍN DE
CACTUS

Tao

Nazaret

Oasis de
Nazaret

Mozaga

FUNDACIÓN
CÉSAR
MANRIQUE

Tahiche

Costa Teguise

San
Bartolomé

taña
ca

Güime

Tías

ARRECIFE

uerto del
armen

Matagorda

Los Pocillos

LANZAROTE

🗡 Beach

🏰 Castle

☆ Tourist attraction

5   10

kilometres

INTRODUCTION

Lanzarote: Desert or Paradise?

Lying only sixty miles off the coast of North Africa, Lanzarote is the most easterly island of the Canary Archipelago and forms part of the Spanish province of Las Palmas. In recent years the number of visitors to the island has increased dramatically, especially from Germany, Scandinavia and the United Kingdom. In 1982, for example, about 182,000 people holidayed in Lanzarote; thirteen years later the figure was approaching 1.5 million. The number of British visitors in the same period increased from 43,000 to 569,000.

One reason for this phenomenal growth is self-evident: daytime temperatures in January and February are normally around 22°C (the low 70°s Fahrenheit) and the sun shines for an average of eight hours per day, thus making the Canary Islands the nearest reliably warm and sunny winter holiday destination for almost the whole of northern Europe. Lanzarote, with its sparse vegetation, proximity to Africa and lack of a high mountain, enjoys considerably more sunshine than many other islands in the archipelago. There is always a breeze to temper the heat of summer, and the nights are dewy but hardly ever cold.

The island is, therefore, an ideal wintering place for the more elderly and those with delicate health, who benefit from the sunshine, the unpolluted atmosphere and the absence of damp. But Lanzarote has equal appeal for the younger holidaymaker. Sunbathing, swimming and watersports are all superb. The clarity of the sea offers some of the best conditions in the northern hemisphere for sub-aqua pursuits, and windsurfers regard the eastern Canaries as one of the top venues in the entire world. Resorts like Puerto del Carmen and Costa Teguise offer restaurants and night life that rival any popular holiday destination in Europe.

But Lanzarote has a great deal more to offer the visitor than just its climate, or even its beaches. The island's unique and spectacular landscape, created by a series of comparatively recent volcanic eruptions, is regularly described as 'lunar' and often strikes visitors at first sight as drab, barren and ugly. Yet, after only a few days, greater familiarity with the island reveals its strange, austere beauty. The stern desolation that covers so much of Lanzarote has a dignity and a silent grandeur that cause many visitors to return again and again. The light plays on the volcanic fields, revealing unexpected colours and textures, while, elsewhere, grotesquely contorted lumps of lava loom hideously, moving witnesses to the inferno that created the tranquillity of Lanzarote today.

To the naturalist, the island is a fascinating habitat of rare plants, a staging post for migratory birds and a breeding ground for thousands of butterflies.

Lanzarote is special in other ways too. Though the local community lives under the constant threat of being overwhelmed by the tourist influx, it has from the beginning got important things right. The water and electricity may fail from time to time, and there may be queues at the airport on Thursdays, but these are things that can and will be remedied. What Lanzarote has avoided with singular success are the irretrievable environmental disasters that mass tourism can bring in its wake – ugly high-rise buildings, advertising hoardings, unsympathetic developments in beauty spots, rubbish tips and environmental pollution. The main resorts are tightly controlled, while three quarters of the island remains quite untouched by tourism and will continue to be so. Thanks largely to the efforts of one man, the artist and architect César Manrique

A spectacular landscape: the valley of Femés

The beach at Puerto del Carmen

(see pp. 61–3), the vernacular architecture of the island has been preserved and most of the new buildings blend harmoniously with the landscape – visitors immediately notice the preponderance of white houses with green or blue paintwork. Less than a year after Manrique's death in 1992 UNESCO declared Lanzarote a Biosphere Reserve, defined as an environment in which man and nature interact to the benefit of both. The designation is intended to ensure that an ecological balance will be retained alongside restricted touristic development, so there are good grounds for the hope that Manrique's beloved island will continue to develop in the way that he would have wished.

The history of the Canary Islands has been one of regular invasion by foreign predators. On Lanzarote, at least, the islanders have managed to accommodate and profit from the advent of mass tourism – perhaps its last and greatest invasion – with dignity, restraint and, always, a warm welcome.

GETTING THERE

By Air

There are no scheduled flights between the UK and Lanzarote at the time of writing. Charter flights to Arrecife depart regularly from most British airports, however, servicing the requirements of package tour operators; and the independent visitor can usually secure a seat on one of these. (Prices vary considerably according to the season.) The great majority of flights are on Thursdays, and flying time is about three hours and 45 minutes. From Heathrow, British Airways and Iberia fly regularly to Madrid, with an onward connecting flight to Arrecife operated by Aviaco daily.

Inter-island flights are operated by Binter Canarias, a subsidiary of Iberia. From Las Palmas de Gran Canaria there are seven flights daily, and four from Tenerife (Norte); in summer there is also a daily flight to Arrecife from Santa Cruz de La Palma.

AIRPORT

Lanzarote's elegant airport, with its distinctive 'wind sculpture' by César Manrique, lies beside the sea at Playa de Guasimeta midway between Arrecife and Puerto del Carmen. Built in 1940 as a military aerodrome, the airport received its first tourist flight in 1946: currently it is being redesigned and expanded, and by the spring of 1998 will be able to accommodate twenty planes on the ground instead of the present eleven.

The number of passengers using the airport has more than doubled in the last decade: during 1995 two million people passed through it and this figure is expected to reach three million within the next fifteen years. Consequently the question of a second runway is being discussed. In the shorter term the present terminal building, designed by Manrique, will be used for inter-island flights while a new larger building, in traditional style but with travelators and direct-boarding tunnels, has been designed by Luis Ibañez and a team of local architects. With this new capacity, the present check-in and baggage handling delays which have become a serious inconvenience on Thursdays (when the majority of U.K. flights arrive and depart) should become a thing of the past.

The airport is well provided with shops selling 'duty free' goods, but as the Canary islands are a duty-free zone, more competitive prices can usually be found in the towns and resorts of the island. Car hire firms and taxis (tel: 814655) operate from the airport and buses to Arrecife run between 07.00 and 19.10 Mon–Fri and from 08.20–17.40 on Saturdays, Sundays and holidays. At the time of writing there is no tourist office. The telephone number for airport information is 815375.

By Sea

Compañía Trasmediterránea S.A. operate a modern, comfortable **ferry**, the *Juan J. Sister*, which sails from Cádiz to Santa Cruz (Tenerife), Las Palmas (Gran Canaria) and Arrecife. This boat leaves Cádiz at 18.00 on Saturdays but does not reach Arrecife until the following Wednesday at 21.00, having called twice at both Santa Cruz and Las Palmas before arriving in Lanzarote. The return voyage to Cádiz is direct, departing from Arrecife at 22.00 on Wednesday and arriving in Cádiz at 11.00 on Friday. In autumn 1996 the price for four people and a car was 102,670 ptas (one way). The agents for Compañía Trasmediterránea in the UK are Southern Ferries, 179 Piccadilly, London W1V 9DB (tel: 0171 491 4968, fax: 0171 491 3502); in Germany, Deutsches Reisebüro Gmbh (DER), Emil von Behringstrasse 6, D-60439 Frankfurt/Main (tel: 069 9588 1772, fax: 069 9588 1774). Their head office is at Obenque 4, Alameda de Osuna, 28042 Madrid (tel: 091 322 9100, fax: 091 322 9110); their Lanzarote office is at José Antonio 90, Arrecife (tel: 811019, fax: 812363).

If you're making for Cádiz, Brittany Ferries (tel: 0990 360360) offer a service between Plymouth and Santander from March to November, and between Portsmouth and Santander from January to March. The Plymouth crossing takes 24 hours, the Portsmouth 30 hours. Prices start from £46 per person one way and from £146 for a car, including the driver. P&O (tel: 0990 980555) sail from Portsmouth to Bilbao throughout the year, taking 36 hours: fares start at £45 per person one way and £145 for a car plus driver. The distance by road from Santander to Cádiz is 1056 km. (656 miles) and from Bilbao to Cádiz 1058 km. (657 miles).

Naviera Armas S.A. (tel: 811019, fax: 812363) run overnight ferries from Las Palmas to Arrecife at 23.50 on Mondays, Wednesdays and Fridays, returning to Las Palmas at 13.00 on Tuesdays, Thursdays and Saturdays. The same company offers a service on the *Volcán de Tindaya* between Playa Blanca (Lanzarote) and Corralejo (Fuerte-ventura), taking 35 minutes (see p. 102 for times); fares are 1,700 ptas each way (children half price), cars 2,500 ptas, motorcycles 1,250 ptas and bicycles 400 ptas. This route is also plied by Fred. Olsen lines (tel: 517266); their ferry *Buganvilla* makes the trip four times daily and offers a free bus service from Puerto del Carmen connecting with two of the crossings.

The **rail** fare from London to Cádiz was (autumn 1996) £240 2nd class return and £361 1st class. Bookings should be made through British Rail International, Victoria Station, London SW1V 1JY (tel: 0171 834 2345, fax: 0171 922 9874).

Lanzarote is a popular port of call for **cruise ships**, many of which anchor off Playa Blanca. In 1995 there were 95 cruise ship arrivals, carrying 48,000 passengers: January and November were the busiest months. Companies including Lanzarote in their itineraries are: P&O Cruises, 77 New Oxford St, London WC1A 1PP (tel: 0171 800 2222, fax: 0171 240 2805), Cunard Line Ltd, South Western House, Canute Road, Southampton, SO14 3NR (tel: 01703 634166, fax: 01703 634500), Fred. Olsen Cruise Lines, Fred. Olsen House, White House Rd, Ipswich, Suffolk IP1 5LL (tel: 01473 292222, fax: 01473 292345), and Costa Cruises, 45/49 Mortimer St, London W1N 8JL (tel: 0171 323 3333, fax: 0171 323 0033).

Citizens of EU countries, the USA and Canada require a valid passport, but no visa. There is no limit on the amount of currency you may take into Spain, but large amounts should be declared on arrival if you are likely to take a sizeable proportion of it out again.

Although Lanzarote is an ideal holiday destination at any time of year, there are seasonal variations in prices. Generally speaking, the high season runs from November through to April (with a peak covering Christmas and the period before Epiphany), and the low season is May-June.

TRAVEL ON LANZAROTE

The variety of sights and scenery on Lanzarote, together with its satisfactorily small size, make hiring a car an attractive option. Add to this the relative cheapness of both car hire and petrol, and it is not surprising that some of the island's roads can feel a little crowded.

In recent years the island government has spent large sums on dramatically improving the road system, and the network of metalled roads is now generally excellent, with bypasses in place around Arrecife and Puerto del Carmen and a new fast road between Yaiza and Playa Blanca. The once alarmingly high accident rate has considerably diminished in consequence. Nevertheless the number of cars on the island continues to climb and careless (or drunken) driving, or simply travelling too fast on the generally narrow roads, is still a problem.

The maximum speed limit on main roads is 90 kmph (100 kmph at some points on the bypasses) and usually 40 kmph in built-up areas. The use of seat belts is compulsory. In common with the European mainland, driving is on the right. In general, traffic has priority from the right unless road markings show otherwise; overtaking is not allowed where there is a single white line down the centre of the road, which is equivalent to a double line in the U.K. The traffic police are empowered to fine motorists on the spot for violations.

La Geria, chapel

Drivers visiting the island in their own cars require, in addition to a national driving licence, a certificate of international insurance ('green card'), and a bail bond; British drivers should adjust their headlamps to deflect the beam for driving on the right.

Breakdown services in an emergency include San Ginés (tel: 520152), Costa Teguise (591982) and Lanzarote (812123), or assistance may be sought from the municipal police in the nearest town. If problems occur with a hired car, however, the hiring agency should be contacted first.

Car Hire

Hiring a car in the Canaries is extremely good value: indeed, their duty-free status makes car hire cheaper than almost anywhere else in Europe. There are a multitude of rental firms on Lanzarote, most of which will deliver a car to the airport or your hotel/apartment for no extra charge. The following table gives an indication of typical car hire prices in pesetas in September 1996.

	1 day	4 days	7 days
Seat Marbella	2050	4950	9450
Opel Corsa/Ford Fiesta	2250	5250	10,500
Ford Escort Atlanta	4600	11,550	23,800
Suzuki Jeep	5200	13,050	26,950
Renault Espace	8100	20,400	42,700

Source: Faycan Rent-a-Car, Lanzarote

To these charges must be added a collision damage waiver (between 1400 and 2300 ptas per day) and 4 per cent local taxes. Further insurances can be added but are probably unnecessary if you have holiday insurance or car insurance cover of your own. Charges are usually for unlimited mileage, though it is wise to check this when hiring. Normally drivers must be over 21, and in theory an International Driving Licence is required, though any national licence is usually accepted in practice.

Some hirers stipulate that their cars should only be driven on metalled roads or the insurance cover is void. This condition is merely made to avoid irresponsible abuses, however, and one has only to see the hordes of small hire cars making their way over the dirt tracks to the Papagayo beaches to appreciate that it is not a rule that needs to be taken too seriously.

PETROL

Petrol on Lanzarote is slightly cheaper than in the UK and three grades are on sale: 97-octane (*súper*) is equivalent to 4-star, 92-octane is known as *normal* and *sin plomo* is unleaded. The island is adequately supplied with petrol stations, most of which stay open on Sundays: the twin stations on the Arrecife bypass are open for 24 hours daily. All but the newest petrol stations are marked on the road maps sold on the island. It is worth remembering that there is no petrol north of Arrieta, nor on the Timanfaya and La Geria roads.

MAPS

Two reasonably good motoring maps are widely available on Lanzarote, published by Distrimapas Telstar and Editorial Yaiza: the former has useful street maps of Arrecife, Puerto del Carmen, Costa Teguise and Playa Blanca on the reverse side. For more detail and a larger scale (1:100,000) the military maps are recommended: two sheets cover the island.

PARKING

In the busier streets of Arrecife and Puerto del Carmen seafront, parking meters have been installed: metered parking spaces are marked with blue lines on the road and the maximum stay permitted is two hours (at 50 ptas per hour in 1996). Exceeding the allotted time may produce a fine, which can be cancelled by paying 250 ptas into the meter. After 20.00 (Monday–Friday) and 14.00 (Saturday) parking in metered places is free. Parking is forbidden not only on yellow/white lines, but also on red/white ones, either of which you may encounter in built-up areas.

Motorcyle Hire

Motorcycles and scooters can be hired from Autos Moreno, Puerto del Carmen (near Maximilian's dance club, tel:

512483, and in the Costa Volcán complex, tel: 510913) and also in the Galeón centre, Playa del Jablillo, Costa Teguise (tel: 592517); also from Sun Bike and Moto, behind the Fariones hotel in Puerto del Carmen (tel: 513440). Prices in September 1996 were 1000 ptas for a day, 2500 ptas for three days and 5000 for a week.

Buses

In the Canary Islands, buses are known as *guaguas* (pronounced 'wahwahs'). Bus services to the less touristic parts of the island are few, but Transportes Lanzarote, SL, based at García Escamez 71, Arrecife (tel: 811546/812458) runs about three dozen buses between Arrecife and Puerto del Carmen from 07.00 to 23.15 at irregular intervals. The journey takes about 30 minutes and the fare is around 180 ptas from any stop. There are also six services on weekdays and three on Sundays from Arrecife to Playa Blanca via Puerto del Carmen (305 ptas each way from Puerto del Carmen to Playa Blanca) and 30 services to Costa Teguise. Information about bus times and services to these and other parts of the island is available from tourist offices (see p.26) and the local press (see pp. 30-1), or from Arrecife bus station at the above address; bus stops within towns are frequent and clearly marked with a blue circle bisected by a red line.

Taxis

Taxis are plentiful in the resorts and drivers carry fixed price lists which are also displayed at the main ranks. Approximate fares (September 1996) for typical journeys from Puerto del Carmen were: airport 1144 ptas, Arrecife 1664, Playa Blanca 3120, Jameos del Agua 4680, Costa Teguise 5200. Taxis will also take you on fixed-price tours of the island: a whole-day excursion, covering most of Lanzarote, will probably cost about 17,000 ptas, while a half day (4-5 hours) driving around the north or the south is 8-10,000. Fares for other typical journeys on the island are Costa Teguise–Arrecife 1040 ptas, Costa Teguise–airport 800, Costa Teguise–Teguise market 1560, Arrecife–airport 800, Playa Blanca–Arrecife 4160, Playa Blanca–airport 3640 and Playa Blanca–Teguise market 4400.

Taxi rank telephone nos. in Puerto del Carmen are:

Lanzarote Airport

513638 (Old Town), 513634 (Fariones), 513656 (Centro Atlántico), 513635 (San Antonio); in Costa Teguise: 590863 (Salinas), 590095 (Teguise Playa), 590160 (Playa Bastián); in Playa Blanca 517136, and in Haría 835031. A 24-hour radio taxi can be called from the rank outside the Arrecife Gran Hotel (803104).

HOTELS AND RESTAURANTS

Accommodation

There are tourist hotels in Arrecife, Puerto del Carmen, Playa Blanca and on the Costa Teguise. The vast majority of visitors to Lanzarote, however, occupy self-catering apartments and villas. This type of accommodation varies from the basic to the relatively luxurious, but the rapid turnover of guests in each apartment tends to make for practical rather than splendid furnishings.

Building work is still going on all over Lanzarote, particularly in the Playa Blanca and Costa Teguise resorts, so some noise from this may be expected. Water is scarce (and expensive – you will be doing Lanzarote a service if you try not to waste it) but cuts are nevertheless rare, despite the ever-increasing numbers of visitors.

Most villas and apartments are booked through package tour companies, of which there are at least 20 in the UK; your travel agent will be able to provide brochures and details. As Puerto del Carmen alone offers 28,000 self-catering beds, it is obviously impossible to provide a full listing of complexes in this book, but independent travellers can obtain a complete list of all the hotels and apartments in the Las Palmas province (which includes Lanzarote) from the Spanish National Tourist Office in London (57–8 St James St, London SW1A 1LD; tel: 0171 499 0901, fax: 0171 629 4257) or from the Patronato de Turismo, Blas Cabrera Felipe s/n, 35500 Arrecife de Lanzarote, Canarias, Spain (tel: 811762, fax: 800080).

Hotels

Hotels on Lanzarote are given a star rating based on the facilities offered; price tariffs are displayed at reception and in each room. To make a booking from outside Lanzarote, the six-figure telephone/fax numbers given below should be prefixed by 00 34 28. The abbreviation 'a.c.' signifies air conditioning.

PUERTO DEL CARMEN

Los Fariones**** Roque del Oeste 1: opened 1966, attractive gardens, small private beach, pool, disco, medical service, a.c.; 237 rooms (tel: 510175, fax: 510202)

Los Fariones Playa**** Acatife 2: aparthotel on the main beach, 2 pools (one heated), tennis, squash, gym, disabled facilities, medical service, a.c.; 231 units (tel: 510175, fax: 510202)

San Antonio**** Avenida de las Playas 84: on the beach, pools (one heated), tennis, gym, disco, children's playground, medical service, a.c.; 331 rooms (tel: 514200, fax: 513080)

Los Jameos Playa**** Playa de los Pocillos: by the beach contiguous with but north of Puerto del Carmen, 2 pools, tennis, squash, archery, gym, water sports; 530 rooms (tel: 511717, fax: 514219)

La Geria**** Playa de los Pocillos: sea front, pools (inc. heated), garden, children's playground, gym, medical service, disabled facilities, a.c.; 242 rooms (tel: 510441, fax: 511919)

Beatriz Playa**** Playa de Matagorda: north of Playa de Los Pocillos, sea front position, pool, mini-golf, tennis, gym, disco, disabled facilities (tel: 512166, fax: 514207)

Sol Lanzarote*** Playa de Matagorda: aparthotel on sea front, 2 pools (one heated), tennis, children's playground; 330 units (tel: 512855, fax: 512803)

Magec** Hierro 8: Puerto del Carmen's only *hostal* is in the Old Town: 14 rooms (tel: 513874)

Self-catering apartments, Puerto del Carmen

COSTA TEGUISE

Meliá Salinas***** *gran lujo*, Playa de las Cucharas: 'private' beach, spectacular atrium with water gardens, pools (one heated), gourmet restaurant, tennis, medical service, disabled facilities, a.c.; 310 rooms (tel: 590040, fax: 590390)

Teguise Playa**** Playa del Jablillo: on the beach, 2 pools (one heated), tennis, squash, gym, children's playground, disabled facilities, medical service, a.c.: 314 rooms (tel: 590654, fax: 590979)

Oasis de Lanzarote**** Playa del Ancla: by the beach, 3 pools (one heated), tennis, squash, gym, casino, disabled facilities, medical service, a.c.; 372 rooms (tel: 590410, fax: 590791)

Beatriz**** Atalaya 3: 2 pools (one heated), tennis, squash, gym, disco, disabled facilities; 345 rooms (tel: 590828, fax: 591785)

Barceló Suites**** Avenida del Mar: aparthotel, sea views, 3 pools, gym, a.c.; 442 units (tel: 591329, fax: 591337)

Lanzarote Bay*** Avenida de las Palmeras 30: aparthotel, pool, garden, tennis, squash, gym, disco, kindergarten; 200 units (tel: 590253, fax: 591366)

Lanzarote Gardens*** Avenida Islas Canarias: aparthotel, pool, tennis, children's playground, disabled facilities; 242 units (tel: 590100, fax: 591784)

PLAYA BLANCA

Lanzarote Princess**** Maciot s/n: heated pools, tennis, squash, children's playground, dancing, a.c.; 407 rooms (tel: 517108, fax: 517011)

Playa Dorada**** urb. Costa de Papagayo: by the beach, 3 pools, water sports, disco, 6 rooms adapted for disabled visitors, medical service, a.c.; 266 rooms (tel: 517120, fax: 517432)

Lanzarote Park*** Playa Flamingo: by the beach, 4 pools, tennis, squash, gym, children's playground; 307 units (tel: 517048, fax: 517348)

ARRECIFE

Lancelot*** Avenida Mancomunidad 9: overlooking beach of Playa del Reducto, pool, piano bar, medical service, a.c.; 110 rooms (tel: 805099, fax: 805039)

Miramar*** Avenida Coll 2: sea front (opposite Castillo de San Gabriel), children's playground, disco, medical service; 90 rooms (tel: 810438, fax: 813366)

LA GRACIOSA

In the main village, Caleta del Sebo, there are three small *pensiones*: **Enriqueta** (tel: 842051), **Girasol Playa** (tel: 842101) and **Betancort** (tel: 842118); self-catering accommodation is also available in **Apartamentos Pescador** (tel: 842036). All are within a short walk from the ferry to Órzola.

Lanzarote has no youth hostels, nor are there any official **camping** sites, but permission to camp on La Graciosa may be obtained from the *ayuntamiento* in Caleta del Sebo (tel/fax: 842000)

Food and Drink

CANARIAN CUISINE

Some Canarian recipes are very old, and all of them, with their very limited ingredients, testify to the islanders' struggle for self-sufficiency in the face of an uncompromising environment. Almost all meat is imported, but kid (*cabrito*), reared on Fuerteventura, and wild rabbit (*conejo salvaje*) appear on more 'rustic' menus.

The traditional food of Lanzarote has a definite bias towards fish and vegetables, and specifically local varieties include:

Fish

atún	tuna
bacalao	salted cod
caballa	Atlantic mackerel
cherne	stone bass
lapas	limpets
lenguado	sole
mero	grouper
sama	red sea bream
vieja	(literally 'old woman'), no translation

Smoked salmon is often described as 'local': there is a

smokehouse at Uga, selling to restaurants and to the public (4,600 ptas per kilo in 1996), but the fish itself originates from mainland rivers.

Vegetables and fruit

acelga	chard or spinach beet
tomates	tomatoes
patatas	potatoes
cebollas	onions
zanahorias	carrots
puerros	leeks
maíz	sweetcorn
calabaza	pumpkin
garbanzos	chickpeas
judías verdes	green beans
plátanos	bananas (from Gran Canaraia)
higos	figs

TRADITIONAL DISHES

gofio   An ancient recipe which seems to have been the staple diet of the Guanche people: consisting of maize, roasted and then ground to flour, it is used as a breakfast cereal, a thickener for soups, as biscuit dough and in dumplings.

puchero canario   A peasant stew whose ingredients may vary, but usually include beef, pork, sausage, chickpeas, maize, pumpkin, potatoes, cabbage, garlic, green beans and saffron. It can be compared to the *cassoulet* of south-west France.

potaje canariense   A thick, nourishing soup with vegetable ingredients very similar to those of *puchero*, but with the addition of tomatoes and with no meat; the soup is usually thickened with *gofio*.

sopa de millo   This is a meat and maize broth, a thinner version of *puchero*.

papas arrugadas   Literally translated, these are 'wrinkled potatoes', and the effect is achieved by boiling unskinned potatoes in a very small quantity of salty water. The salt forms a crust on the skins of the potatoes: they are often served as *tapas* in bars, where they are dipped in piquant *mojo* sauce.

salsa de mojo rojo   (red *mojo* sauce) This is a mixture of garlic, paprika, cumin seed, olive oil, thyme and vinegar with water added as a dilutant. It is commonly served with *papas arrugadas* or with salted fish: the latter combination is called *sancocho*. To make the green variety, *salsa de mojo verde*, which is often served alongside the red version, finely chopped coriander leaves replace the paprika. Both variants of *mojo* sauce are unique to the Canary Islands.

arroz cubana   A Cuban import, boiled rice with added garlic and fried onion, topped with sliced bananas sautéed in butter, now thought of as traditional Lanzarote fare.

frangollos   Corn-based milk pudding, flavoured with honey, brandy and/or cinnamon.

torrijas   Sweet fritters of maize flour, with aniseed and honey.

plátanos fritos   Bananas are available in quantity from the plantations of Gran Canaria and Tenerife, and fried bananas are a favourite dessert; they are not coated in batter but fried in oil, then dusted with sugar and sprinkled with lemon juice and brandy; they are also served baked with almonds, chocolate powder and cream (*bienmesabe*).

Another dessert you may meet is a delicious cheese pudding – a confection of goat's cheese, cream, egg, caraway and caramel called *pudín de queso fresco*.

Since the time of the Guanches (p.47) goat's **cheese** has been made on the island. The Quesería El Faro (tel/fax: 173113), 4 km out of Teguise on the Mozaga road, was established more than fifty years ago by the family who still run it, and makes 3,000 litres of home-produced goat's milk into cheese every day. This is sold in shops throughout the island, as well as from the factory and at Teguise market. Three stages of maturity are on sale: *fresco* (white and crumbly), *semi-curado* (yellow, denser texture but mild in flavour) and *curado* (a hard, golden cheese which keeps well); there is also *ahumado*, cured and then smoked over prickly pear leaves.

WINE

Wines and spirits from all over the world can be purchased on Lanzarote at 'duty-free' prices, but it would be a shame not to sample the local *malvasía* while on the island. This is the 'malmsey', 'canary' or 'sacke' of Shakespeare; it is produced from the vineyards of La Geria, San Bartolomé and the Mozaga-Tao area, using the local *macetas* method: planting the vines in a pit which is then partially filled in with porous black lava granules (*picón*) which feed any moisture available down to the roots. Two brands of local wine are widely available, the award-winning El Grifo (from family vineyards on the eastern edge of Masdache which have been producing for over two centuries), and Mozaga. Both vineyards produce red wine (*tinto*), rosé (*rosado*), and dry (*seco*), medium (*semi-seco*) and sweet (*moscatel*) whites; in 1994 El Grifo introduced Lanzarote's first champagne. All these wines are heady and potent (up to 17 per cent proof), with a strong and unusual flavour that in the whites (which are a deep yellow in colour) reminds some people of sherry. The *semi-secos* have a raisin nose and are not as strong as the *secos* – all are improved by chilling. Lanzarote's production of *malvasía* grapes hovers around 1.5 million kilos per annum; unlike many other wine-producing areas, the island has never been plagued by phylloxera.

In the La Geria region several vineyards offer opportunities for tasting and buying their wines. El Grifo, the oldest of them, has opened a museum of tools, presses and barrels and other implements of viticulture (open Mon–Fri, 10.00–18.00); it also sells its own wines and those of the neighbouring islands.

The Canaries also produce **rum** (notably Ron Arehucas from Las Palmas) and a banana liqueur called *cobana*. The local **mineral water** is Chafarí, from a spring on the eastern flank of the Famara massif.

Restaurants

There are over 600 restaurants on Lanzarote. The majority of them are in Puerto del Carmen, Costa Teguise and Arrecife and offer an international menu, with an emphasis on the staples of tourist catering in mainland Spain: *paella*, *gazpacho*, *tortillas*, asparagus dishes and '*flan*'. However it is quite easy to find places which serve local dishes, both in the resorts and elsewhere on the island. For self-caterers, a book of Canarian recipes is widely on sale and the ingredients are readily available.

As in any holiday area, most eating places are willing to serve meals from mid-morning until late; all have menus (often multilingual) with prices displayed outside, and tend to serve generous – often over-generous – portions. Traditional (late) Spanish eating hours are not generally observed: arrive for lunch at 13.30 or dinner at 20.30 and you may find the more popular restaurants already full.

A minority of restaurants stand out from the crowd, either for their authentic Canarian cuisine or for their very high standards: some of them can stand comparison with the best in Europe and have prices to match. A helpful restaurant guide is the *Dolphin Guide to Eating and Drinking in Lanzarote*, published in Puerto del Carmen in 1996.

A selection of recommended restaurants is listed below:

ARRECIFE

Casa Ginory, Juan de Quesada 7: on the NE corner of Charco de San Ginés, fresh local fish; open 13.00–16.00, 20.00–23.00, closed Saturday evening and all day Sunday (tel: 804046)

Castillo San José (see p.63): good food stylishly served in magnificent castle setting overlooking the sea; open 13.00–15.45, 20.00–23.00 (tel: 812321)

El Almirante, Playa del Cable: on the seashore, imaginative menu, good wine list; open 11.00–23.30 (tel: 805985)

Marisquería Abdon, Canalejas 54; near town centre, reasonably priced seafood, take-away service; open 12.30–16.00, 19.00–23.00 (tel: 814558)

ARRIETA

El Charcón, fish restaurant right by the slipway, very popular on Sundays; open 10.30–20.45, closed Wed. (tel: 835630)

El Lago, on the coast road to Punta Mujeres; natural indoor sea water pool containing 'seafood'; open 12.00–22.00 (12.00–17.00 Sun.), closed Tues. (tel: 835616)

Miguel's, on the quay, full of character, fresh fish at reasonable prices; open 12.00–21.00 Tues.–Sat. (12.00–17.00) Sun., closed Mon. (tel: 835225)

LA CALETA (DE FAMARA)

El Risco, stunning views of Famara cliffs and La Graciosa from César Manrique's former holiday home (restaurant adorned with his pictures); Canarian cuisine, welcoming atmosphere; open for lunch and dinner (no phone)

CASAS DE EL GOLFO

Lago Verde, spotless new restaurant, choose your own freshly caught fish (tel: 173311)

Plácido, on the shore, relaxed, unpretentious and very popular fish restaurant (tel: 173302)

COSTA TEGUISE

Dos Amigos, Playa Bastián: busy Tex-Mex restaurant, with young clientele, authentic Mexican food and exciting cocktails; open 18.30–23.30 (tel: 591145)

La Jordana, by Lanzarote Bay aparthotel; fashionable restaurant with good reputation for cuisine and service, international (and occasionally royal) clientele; open 12.00–16.00, 18.30–23.30, closed Sun. and all Sept. (tel: 590328)

Mahatma Cote, Avenida del Jablillo: genuine Indian restaurant, specialising in *karai* (stir-fried) dishes, friendly service; open 19.00–23.15, closed Thurs. (tel: 591967)

Neptuno, Peninsula del Jablillo; excellent food in attractive room with fountain; good *paella* and fondues; open 12.00–16.00, 19.00–23.00, closed Sun. (tel: 590378)

El Pescador, Pueblo Marinero: interior walls clad in elaborately carved wooden bas-reliefs depicting the rural and undersea life of Lanzarote (the work of José Domingo Abreut); good food and friendly atmosphere; open 12.00–15.30, 18.30–23.30 (tel: 590874)

FEMÉS

Casa Emiliano, glorious views to Lobos and Fuerteventura, home cooking by village family, busy in summer; open 11.30–22.30 (tel: 830223)

HARÍA

Casa'l Cura, Nueva 1; reasonably priced buffet lunch served in old Canarian house; open 12.00–17.00 (tel: 835556)

MACHER

El Pozo, Camino de la Molina 11: panoramic views, barbecued meats and home-made pasta cooked by Italian chef; open 18.30–23.30, closed Mon. (tel: 512454)

MOZAGA

Casa Museo El Campesino, self-service buffet of local specialities in new restaurant by Manrique's monument (see p. 97), local wines; open 12.30–16.30 (tel: 520136)

NAZARET

El Oasis, Golondrinas 6; international menu, poolside barbecues, live music Sun.; open 11.00–23.30 (tel: 845673)

ÓRZOLA

Punta Fariones, Quemadita 8: fresh seafood near the quay; open 08.00–22.00 (tel: 842558)

The harbour at Órzola

PLAYA BLANCA

Almacén de la Sal, Avenida Maritima 20: former salt warehouse, carefully restored, Canarian and Basque dishes, piano music and occasional flamenco; open 10.00–24.00 (tel: 517885)

Casa Joaquín, Playa Flamingo: above the beach, international cuisine, cocktails, live music nightly; open 11.00–23.00 (tel: 517438)

El Horno de la Abuela, Trasero Paseo Maritimo 10; behind the sea front, Castilian cuisine in intimate setting; open 13.00–16.00, 18.30–23.00 (tel: 517825)

PUERTO CALERO

El Bar del Club, on the marina with views of Fuerteventura; fresh fish, good salads, barbecue with live music Fri.; open 12.00–23.00, closed Mon. (tel: 510015)

PUERTO DEL CARMEN

La Cañada, César Manrique 3; freshly cooked dishes include fish baked in sea salt prepared by chef-owner; open 12.30–24.00 (tel: 512108)

El Fondeadero, overlooking the harbour; impeccable cooking by catering college students; open 12.00–16.00, 19.00–23.00, closed Monday lunch and all day Sun. (tel: 511465)

Montmartre, Jameos 5; friendly small French bistro, very popular; open 19.00–23.00 (tel: 520773)

El Sardinero-Casa Tino, by the harbour; family run, Canarian food, glorious view; open 09.00–23.00 (tel: 511933)

El Varadero, by the harbour in a converted boathouse; marine decor and very fresh shellfish; open 11.00–23.30 (tel: 513162)

TEGUISE

Acatife, San Miguel 4; elegant dining room, Canarian and international cooking, busy on Sundays; open 12.00–16.00, 19.00–23.30 (09.00–16.00 Sun.), closed Mon. and 15 May–15 June (tel: 845037)

Casa Cristóbal, just outside town on the Arrecife road,

extensive views, international menu; open 11.00–16.00, 19.00–23.30, closed Tues. and 15 June–15 July (tel: 845295)
La Cantina, León y Castillo 8; old house centred on patio; Spanish cuisine, open 11.00–23.30 (08.00–17.30 Sun.), closed Mon. and 24 May–15 June (tel: 845109)

TIMANFAYA

El Diablo, Manrique-designed with a devil's frying-pan motif, magnificent volcanic views, meat grilled over the heat of the volcano, local wine; open for lunch (organised excursion parties in the evening tel: 840056)

YAIZA

Jardines La Era, El Barranco 3; well signposted in the village, 17th-century farmstead, one of only three buildings in Yaiza to survive the 18th-century eruption; restored and converted by César Manrique, who jointly owned it with Luis Ibañez; authentic local dishes and home-bottled Lanzarote wine; open 13.00–16.00, 19.00–23.00 (tel: 830016)
El Volcán, Plaza de Los Remedios; busy restaurant opposite the church, reasonable prices: open 08.00–16.00, closed Saturdays (tel: 830156).

Jardines La Era restaurant at Yaiza

Eating out in Puerto del Carmen

Nightlife

Puerto del Carmen remains the centre of nightlife on Lanzarote, though Costa Teguise now offers strong competition. In the older resort popular discos include **Dreams** (very large), **Waikiki**, **Hippodrome**, **Big Apple**, **Charlie's** (young clientele) and **Maximilian's**; most of these are in the Centro Atlántico on the sea front road, which is the hub of Puerto del Carmen's club scene. 'Fun Pubs' include **Cervecería Tropical**, **Bubble's** (for karaoke) and **Amadeus**, with a party every night. Many of the bars along the 'strip' offer satellite television (particularly appealing to football fans): **Lineker's** has eight large screens. Among the bars in the Old Town is **Bourbon Street**, where dancers of all ages are treated to '50s and '60s music. Cabaret shows and dancing to a live band can be enjoyed at **Moonlight Bay** by the beach at Playa de los Pocillos: it is open from 21.00 whereas most discos do not really get going until midnight.

At Costa Teguise **Memphis Blues** and **Saxo** are lively music bars; both are on the Avenida del Jablillo, and both have dance floors. **Treble**, near the Lanzarote Gardens aparthotel, is a 'fun pub' with live entertainment, dancing, karaoke and TV screens for football enthusiasts. Apart from the discos in the large hotels, Playa Blanca's nightlife is largely centred on bars: the **Buccaneer** in the Punta

Jameos del Agua

Limones centre offers karaoke and a large TV screen; also at Punta Limones is the exotic **Oca Loca Disco Garden**, open till 05.00. **Susan's Place** on Playa Flamingo beach is a disco-pub with occasional live music.

Arrecife is lively at night, especially in the central La Destila area. Among the music bars on calle José Antonio are **La Antigua** (no. 62) and **Menta** (no. 74). **Pub La Fábrica** at no. 64 has a 'yuppie' image: the latest music is played in arty surroundings (the paintings are for sale). At the time of writing, **La Naos**, next to Puerto Naos, is the newest nightspot to attract the 'beautiful people': housed in a marquee with an open-air terrace, it has five bars and dancing indoors and out and opens from 23.00 on Thurs–Sat.

A cabaret consisting of displays of Canarian dancing can be enjoyed at **Jameos del Agua** on Tuesday and Saturday nights, when the grotto is transformed into an unusually atmospheric nightclub (see p.119).

The island's only **casino** is at the Centro Comercial Pequeña Europa, Puerto del Carmen. It is open from 20.00 to 04.00; formal dress is not required, but the minimum age for entry is 18 years (passport confirmation required at the door).

PRACTICAL INFORMATION

Tourist Information

Lanzarote's tourist authority is based in Arrecife's former *parador*, which also houses the Red Cross headquarters, just east of the skyscraper Gran Hotel. (It and the adjoining library are worth visiting for a glimpse of the colourful murals by the young César Manrique they contain, which are often reproduced on posters and postcards.) The main tourist information office, sited in a small building in the park a little further east, dispenses maps, leaflets and advice on accommodation, transport and attractions; it is open from 09.00–13.00 and 17.30–19.30 Mon–Fri and 09.00–13.00 on Saturdays (tel/fax: 811860). On Puerto del Carmen sea front, tourist information is available from an octagonal wooden kiosk above the middle of the beach (same opening hours as the Arrecife office, tel: 515337), while at Playa Blanca there is a small office by the ferry terminal, open 10.00–18.00 Mon–Fri only (tel: 517794). At the time of writing, there was no tourist office at the airport or at Costa Teguise.

Time

Time in the Canaries is one hour behind the rest of Spain; it is therefore the same as GMT in winter, but from the last Sunday in March to the last Sunday in October is an hour ahead.

Banks and Currency

The currency of Lanzarote is the Spanish peseta. Banks are usually open from 08.00–14.00 Mon–Fri and 08.00–12.00 on Saturdays, but most hotels, apartment complexes and exchange offices will change foreign currency outside these hours. Eurocheques and credit cards can be used at banks for obtaining cash and are widely accepted in restaurants. If your credit cards are lost or stolen, emergency telephone numbers to ring are: Mastercard and Visa, 91 519 2100; Eurocard, 91 519 6000; and American Express, 91 572 0303.

Public Holidays

In addition to the movable feasts of Good Friday, Easter Day and Corpus Christi, Spain has public holidays on 1 January, 6 January (Epiphany), 1 May (Labour Day), 30 May (Canary Day), 24 June (St John the Baptist), 25 July (Santiago), 15 August (Assumption), 12 October (Columbus Day), 1 November (All Saints'), 8 December (Immaculate Conception) and Christmas Day. Several other Saints' Days are celebrated locally (see pp. 67–8).

Post

Postal services to and from other parts of the world are not, in general, particularly swift. In late 1996 the cost of posting letters and postcards from Lanzarote to other parts of Spain was 32 ptas, to other EU countries 65 ptas and to the USA 87 ptas. Stamps (*sellos*) are usually available from the same sources as postcards, also from tobacconists and post offices (*correos*). The main post office in Arrecife is on Generalisimo Franco (the seafront road); it is open 08.00–14.00 Mon–Fri, 08.00–13.00 Saturday (tel: 800673). Other post offices are: Puerto del Carmen, Juan Carlos I s/n (Old Town), open 09.00–13.00 Mon–Sat (tel: 510381); Costa Teguise, Avenida Islas Canarias (C.C. Las Maretas), open 10.00–13.00 Mon–Fri, 10.00–12.00 Sat (tel: 842144); Playa Blanca, calle Papagayo (behind the Black and Amber pub),

A typical house at Yaiza

open 09.00–13.00 Mon–Sat (tel: 830011). Post boxes on Lanzarote are yellow; Poste Restante should be addressed to *Lista de Correos*, followed by the relevant town.

Telephones

International telephone calls can be made from all kiosks, and phoning home is simple: instructions in several languages are displayed in every kiosk. The full range of peseta coins is accepted, also credit cards and phone cards (*tarjetas telefónicas*) which are sold at post offices, newsagents and some other shops. It may be more convenient to make your call from a manned multi-booth *telefónica*: these are open during normal shopping hours and payment is made to the attendant after completing the call (you can also send faxes from them).

All telephone calls are charged at a reduced rate from 22.00–08.00 Mon–Fri, from 14.00 on Saturdays and all day on Sunday. To call the U.K. from Lanzarote dial 0744, then the number you require with the initial zero omitted (other international dialling codes are: Germany 0749, France 0733, the Netherlands 0731, Ireland 07353, USA 071). To make a reverse charge call to the U.K. via a BT operator, call 900 990044. To phone or fax Lanzarote from the U.K. dial 00 3428, then the local 6-digit number.

Health and Medical Care

Spain is a member of the EU and visitors from other member countries who have brought the necessary documentation (a form E111 for the UK) can claim free medical treatment. To do this, you must take the form in advance to the Social Security Office (Instituto Nacional de Previsión), Fajardo 2, Arrecife, where you will be given vouchers which can be used at some of the clinics on the island. Standard holiday insurance should cover most kinds of medical treatment, however, though it is sensible to confirm this before treatment. In **Puerto del Carmen**, medical assistance can be obtained from the Salus Clinic at Avenida de las Playas 5 (tel: 513271, or for 24-hour emergency doctor and ambulance Freephone 900 100 144); the Deutsche Britische Klinik, Los Pocillos (tel: 511960 or 592125 for 24-hour emergency doctor), and the British Skandinavian Clinic, Avenida de Las Playas 10 (tel: 514030 – 24-hour ambulance service). In **Costa Teguise** the Salus Clinic (tel: 592026), next to the Lanzarote Gardens aparthotel, offers a 24-hour medical service on Freephone 900 100 144 and the Clínica Costa Teguise (tel: 591621/591014) is open 10.30–12.00 Mon–Fri and 10.00–12.00 on Saturdays in the Los Zocos complex. **Playa Blanca** has a Salus Clinic by the Lanzarote Park Hotel (tel: 517568 or Freephone 900 100 144 for emergencies) and the Deutsche Klinik in the Yaiza complex (tel: 517938). The island's main hospital is at Carretera Tinajo, Arrecife (tel: 801636). To call a hospital ambulance in an emergency, phone 812062/812222, or the Red Cross on 814866.

The British Dental Clinic at Los Topes 3, Bajo, Tías (tel: 833573) is open for routine appointments 09.30–17.00 Mon–Fri, but will treat emergencies at other times. Reciprocal NHS arrangements do *not* cover dental treatment.

A **pharmacy** (*farmacia*) is always marked with a green Maltese cross. They can give simple medical advice and first aid as well as selling medicines and dispensing prescriptions. In Puerto del Carmen *farmacias* can be found in Roque Nublo (Old Town) and in the Chafarí and Aquarium complexes; in Costa Teguise by the Pueblo Marinero; in Playa Blanca at El Botiquín. There are pharmacies in Yaiza and Tías, and nine in Arrecife, two of them in Léon y Castillo, the main shopping street. Most *farmacias* open from 09.15–13.00 and 16.30–20.00 (mornings only on Saturdays), but a rota system ensures that one will be open until 22.00 every day; one in Arrecife stays open all night. Notices on any *farmacia* door will tell you which to visit outside normal hours.

Lavatories

It is acceptable to use the facilities of bars, restaurants and hotels without buying a drink. The standard of lavatories on Lanzarote is high on the whole, the design of those at the restaurant in Castillo San José being particularly stunning.

Tipping

In general a small tip is expected in restaurants even when a service charge has been added to the bill. As everywhere in the world, taxi drivers and hairdressers expect a tip of 5–10 per cent, and maids, hotel porters and cloakroom attendants appreciate a small gratuity.

Electricity

Lanzarote has two conspicuous wind farms: a small one on Monte Mina behind Arrecife and a very much larger establishment at Los Valles, on the central spine of the northern part of the island. The Los Valles *Parque Eólico*, visible from both east and west coasts, is the second largest in Spain, with forty-eight windmills producing 1,200,000 KW of electricity per month.

The voltage on Lanzarote is 220 (as opposed to 240 in the UK); two-pin plugs are in general use and an adaptor is needed for British appliances. The emergency telephone number of the electricity company, UNELCO, is 800384.

Water

All mains water on Lanzarote is desalinated and, during the last thirty years five desalination plants have been constructed on the island. Recycled water is used for watering crops and garden plants: a complicated irrigation system, reaching most parts of the island, has been developed by the water authority, INALSA. As elsewhere in Spain, the common practice is to drink bottled mineral water, either *con gas* (fizzy) or *sin gas* (still), which is inexpensive and widely available: the local spring water, Chafarí, comes from the eastern slope of the Famara massif.

Newspapers and Radio

Foreign newspapers are widely available in the resorts, usually a day late, and local dailies such as *Canarias 7* provide island and international news for Spanish speakers. The quarterly English-language version of the well-established island journal *Lancelot* is edited from León y Castillo 109, Arrecife (tel: 512026, fax: 510179) and is an invaluable source of practical and tourist information as well as features on island life, history, culture and much else of interest. A free magazine, *Canarian Gazette* (tel: 802787, fax: 800845), also contains useful current information: it is circulated to hotels, apartment complexes and some shops.

Radio Lanzarote (90.7 FM) and Radio Insular de Lanzarote (96.8 FM) broadcast only in Spanish, but Radio Volcán (89.7 FM) has English programmes between 17.00 and 18.00 Mon–Fri and 14.00–15.00 on Sundays. Radio

Europa (102.7 FM) broadcasts in German 24 hours daily, and the World Service of the BBC can be found on various shortwave frequencies at different times of day, including 12.095, 15.070 and 17.705 MHz. On television, Euro Diario on Channel 2 has news in English, French and German at 13.00 Mon–Fri.

Consulates

The nearest consulates are in Las Palmas in Gran Canaria. Mr Peter Nevitt, the British Consul, has an office at Edificio Cataluña, Luis Morote 6-3, which opens 08.00–14.30 on weekdays (tel: 262508, fax: 267774 – these numbers can be used out of hours in an emergency). He visits Lanzarote in February, May, August and November, when he opens a temporary office in the Hotel Los Fariones, Puerto del Carmen. Other nations with consular representation in Las Palmas include France (tel: 282371), Germany (tel: 275700) the Netherlands (tel: 242382) and the USA (tel: 271259). These numbers can be dialled without a prefix from Lanzarote. Ireland is represented in Tenerife (tel: 922 245671).

Religious Services

Regular Catholic masses are held in most churches – see the local press for times. Bilingual (English and Spanish) mass is celebrated at 11.00 and 19.00 each Sunday in the church of N.S. del Carmen near the harbour at Puerto del Carmen, with an Anglican communion service at 12.15. Sunday services for Anglicans are also held at the Playa Blanca church at 18.00 and at the church of Vera Cruz, Teguise, at 09.00. The chaplain of St Laurence in Lanzarote is the Rev. John Jenkin (tel: 514241). Masses in German are celebrated on Saturdays at 17.00 in Puerto del Carmen and at 19.00 in Playa Blanca, and on Sundays in the Hotel Meliá Salinas in Costa Teguise. The Evangelical Christian church holds services at 20.00 on Saturdays at La Hoya commercial centre, Puerto del Carmen, and at 11.00 on Sundays at the Lanzarote Beach Club, Costa Teguise. There is no synagogue on the island.

Property Purchase

The Canary Islands are an offshore tax haven and house prices are rising. Property for sale, including timeshare, is plentiful on Lanzarote and many visitors from northern Europe continue to find the idea of a permanent base on the island attractive, even if they use it for only a week or two a year. Each issue of both *Lancelot* and *Canarian Gazette* contains useful guidelines on purchasing procedure, while strongly advising that negotiations should only be conducted through an accredited estate agent and an independent solicitor. If you are considering buying land for future building, bear in mind that permission for this may not be granted: applications to build have to be submitted to the relevant town hall (*ayuntamiento*), accompanied by exact plans signed by a locally registered architect, and are scrutinized with great thoroughness.

During the last decade, timeshare ownership in the Canaries has become very popular, especially with the British. Whilst in Lanzarote you may find (particularly if you are a couple over 25) that you are accosted by sales representatives who may offer extravagant inducements merely for agreeing to visit the development they are trying to sell. There is of course no harm in going along with this, *provided* you sign nothing and do not pay even the most minimal deposit until you are sure you want to be committed. Successful timeshare complexes include the still expanding Lanzarote Beach Club at Costa Teguise, offering 5-star accommodation and facilities, Oasis Lanz Club, also at Costa Teguise, and Club del Carmen at Los Pocillos.

Emergencies

Useful telephone numbers in an emergency are: police 091, ambulance 061, Guardia Civil (traffic police) 062, Fire Brigade 080.

GEOLOGY AND CLIMATE

The Canary Islands, together with the Azores and the Cape Verde Islands, are part of the mid-Atlantic ridge, thought to have been formed by volcanic eruptions in the Tertiary period, around twenty million years ago. The total area of Lanzarote is 795 sq. km, of which almost three-quarters is covered with volcanic lava: there are over one hundred craters on the island. In the main, the coasts are rocky and precipitous in the north and west, and more sandy and shelving in the south and east.

Almost certainly, Lanzarote and the five small islets around it were once joined to the African continent, as part of a great cape off the coast of southern Morocco, which today is only some sixty miles away. This theory derives support from such facts as the composition of the sand on the island, which is the same as that of the Sahara, and by the discovery on Lanzarote of the fossilized eggs of the now extinct flightless bird *Aepyornis* (elephant bird) which originated in Madagascar. There is also plenty of evidence that Lanzarote was once joined to Fuerteventura, with the island of Lobos as a bluff of high ground in between the two. La Bocaina, the strait which now divides them, is less than 100 metres deep, whereas the water is twice this depth between Lanzarote and the Roque del Este off the northern end of the island.

Lanzarote comprises two major volcanic massifs, Famara-Guatifay in the north and Los Ajaches in the south. These are linked by a sandy plain dotted with minor volcanic craters left by the numerous eruptions that have marked the island's history. It was not until the eighteenth century that a third range of mountains, those of the Timanfaya National Park, appeared.

The Famara massif plunges abruptly into the sea in a 23-km rampart of cliffs, rising in places to 600 metres high, which form the island's north-western coast. The highest point on the island, Peñas del Chache (670 m.), rises near the centre of the massif and the range is at its most precipitous in this area.

Volcanic eruptions have occurred on Lanzarote through-out its history, and Monte Corona, just east of the Famara massif, is at least 4000 years old. Lava from its eruption flowed north-east to form the *malpaís* (badlands) of Corona, which meet the sea most famously at Jameos del Agua. The cavern here, and at the nearby Cueva de los Verdes (see pp. 117–18), are sections of the world's longest 'volcanic tube', the Atlántida Tunnel, which is 6 km long and stretches out under the sea for 1.6 km: its full extent was explored for the first time in July 1992.

The older, southerly massif of Los Ajaches is less dramatic and more rounded than that of Famara. Here the highest point is the Atalaya de Femés (608 m.), on the

Landslip near Femés

southern slopes of which a quarry clearly displays the dramatic strata of black basalt. To the south-east rises the slightly lower Hacha Grande, from which several 'tongues' branch out towards the southern coast; these culminate in the low sandstone cliffs which separate the Papagayo beaches.

Geologically, the most interesting mountain range on the island is of course the youngest: Timanfaya, formed in historic times over a period of six years from 1730 and 1736 when more than thirty volcanoes were in full activity. The eruptions here laid waste an area of some 174 sq. km., burying ten villages as well as much of the most fertile agricultural land on the island. The area has been a national park since 1974 and forms the major tourist attraction on Lanzarote. At the top of the Islote de Hilario, the temperature a few centimetres below ground is around 100°C – thirteen metres below the surface it reaches 600°C. There has apparently been no significant reduction in these temperatures in the last two hundred years. Entertaining demonstrations can be seen here – brushwood bursts spontaneously into flames and water poured into a sunken pipe emerges within seconds as a fierce geyser of steam. The 'moonscape' of volcanic cones and vast ash-covered plains in the area is virtually devoid of vegetation and often strewn with boulders and stones ejected from the volcanic craters and known as *lapilli* or *picón*. The solidified lava flows are twisted into coils like rope or piled up like petrified waves. Where the lava flow met the sea, black bridges and

Islote de Hilario, Timanfaya – flames from the volcano

promontories have been formed by the erosion of the waves. The most spectacular instances of the sea's struggle to recover its lost terrain can be seen at Los Hervideros on the south-west coast.

In 1824 a further volcanic eruption occurred in the same area, at Tinguatón. This lasted only two months and was minor compared with the earlier series; boiling sea water inundated the countryside, but most of the land affected had already been devastated by the upheavals at Timanfaya. This eruption did, however, form a vast crater, at the bottom of which is the so-called Cueva del Diablo which has been explored to a depth of 80 metres and is the deepest crater in the Canaries.

West of here is the spectacular phenomenon of El Golfo, where the sea invaded the crater of a volcano; the water, trapped there when the sea receded, has now lost its saltiness and become a silent, bright green lagoon. At El Golfo the cliffs are of sandstone, and are remarkable for their spectacular striations.

Geologically, Lanzarote is one of the world's most exciting islands: the volcanic devastation continues to dominate the lives of its inhabitants but has also become an important attraction for visitors. The excellent Interpretation Centre at Mancha Blanca (see p. 89) provides a great deal of useful information about the island's geology.

Climate

Although Lanzarote lies at 28°N (the same latitude as Delhi and New Orleans) and is only 60 miles from the coast of North Africa, its climate is tempered by the cold 'Canaries Current'. This means that the temperature of the sea is lower than might be expected at this latitude and, accordingly, summers are warm rather than blisteringly hot.

In summer the weather is usually dry and sunny – up to 11 hours of sunshine a day – with temperatures between 18°C and 28°C. The hottest days occur when dry air from the Sahara is blown over Lanzarote on the easterly wind known as the sirocco (locally *calima*). Fine dust particles are carried from the desert in these conditions, but the air becomes relatively humid on its journey westward, due to its passage over the cool Atlantic.

Because of the purity of the atmosphere the intensity of the sun's rays can be extremely high, particularly between 11.00 and 15.00.

Winters are mild, with temperatures varying between 14°C and 21°C; they are also relatively sunny – six hours daily is an average. Occasionally, Atlantic depressions may disturb the usually reliable weather, especially in December and January, but storms and prolonged rain are not common. The prevailing winds are the north-east trades originating from the almost permanent anti-cyclone off the Azores; these blow most strongly between March and August, which, for this reason, is the most popular season for windsurfing. East and south-east winds bring dry conditions, and westerlies herald rain. Low cloud which settles on the Riscos (cliffs) de Famara sustains a colony of rare plants, and the dewfall every third night or so is vital to Lanzarote's agriculture.

The annual rainfall on Lanzarote is one-fifth of that in London, but there can be occasional sub-tropical squalls or storms: in December 1991 there were flooding problems in several parts of the island. Lanzarote's winter climate attracts a large number of visitors from northern Europe and is warmer than, say, Majorca, the Costa del Sol or the South of France; while there may be few completely cloudless days, there are equally few when the sun does not shine at all. Sea temperatures range from 17°C in January to 22°C in August, September and October.

CLIMATIC TABLE

	average temp. °C	rainfall mm	wind speed kmph
January	17.0	50.8	23
February	18.8	1	19
March	19.7	11.6	28
April	20.5	7	24
May	25.2	0.4	22
June	25.2	0	27
July	25.5	0	30
August	25.6	0	30
September	25.8	0	28
October	25.2	42.3	19
November	22.3	1.8	14
December	18.8	2.6	19

NATURAL HISTORY

Lanzarote's unusual landscape presents a rather difficult environment for the usual range of Atlantic plants and creatures: many 'modified' sub-species have therefore evolved and are now protected by the island's Reserve of the Biosphere status. An active conservation group, El Guincho, has operated on Lanzarote for the last six years, taking up issues ranging from the erosion of sand dunes by jeep safaris to the shooting of shearwaters for the table. El Guincho can be contacted at Apartado de Correos 365, Arrecife (tel: 815432, fax: 815430). Their office is in the Red Cross building (former *parador*) on the seafront and is open from 09.00–13.00 Monday to Friday.

Flowering Plants

Although Lanzarote is such a dry island, and much of it is devoid of vegetation, there are nevertheless many exciting plants to be discovered by the amateur botanist. The most rewarding time to look for them is, of course, the spring, but a spell of rain at any time of year encourages flowering almost as much as the season.

The vast majority of Lanzarote's plants are found in the northern district of Haría, and especially on the slopes of the Famara massif. Almost all are, of necessity, xerophilous: that is, adapted to grow in drought conditions. On the coast they tend to be halophytes: plants which can survive in very salty soil. Apart from the indigenous plants, trees and shrubs, there are numerous others which have been introduced from the Spanish mainland, Central America and other parts of the world. Obvious examples of these are agave, prickly pear, eucalyptus, poinsettia, morning glory and tree mallow.

In addition to all these, two hundred species of lichen and fifteen kinds of moss grow on the lava. The whitish-green lichen crust on the rocks which line the 'Ruta de los Volcanes' at Timanfaya is reputed to form the staple diet of rabbits. At Órzola, a vivid red and orange carpet of lichens

(Above) House at Yaiza (Below) Jardines de la Era, Yaiza

View of Yaiza

Timanfaya National Park

makes a strong contrast to the white sand, while, at Masdache, the fields of clinker are adorned by rich growths of grey lichen, setting off large clumps of mesembryanthemum.

The following list does not claim to be a full inventory of Lanzarote's flora, but may serve to give an indication of the wide variety of plants that can be found.

Aeonium balsamiferum   large member of the houseleek family with yellow flowers smelling like balsam; Riscos de Famara, Haría, very rare.

Aeonium lancerottense   large houseleek whose green leaves are often edged with red or orange; pink flowers; locally common in the northern part of the island.

Aichryson tortuosum   small creeping succulent with gold flowers; Haría, Riscos de Famara, Mirador del Río, up to 700 m.

Andryala cheiranthifolia   bright yellow dandelion-like flower-heads borne on a woody plant with narrow serrated leaves; Haría region.

Argyranthemum ochroleucum   pale yellow chrysanthemum found on the cliffs of Famara, Peñas de Chache, Haría and inland between Arrecife and Famara.

Artemisia canariensis   small grey-leaved aromatic shrub with brownish-yellow flowers; found on low ground; '*incienso*' in Spanish.

Asteriscus intermedius   yellow daisy with grey stems; locally common on Famara Massif and near Jameos del Agua.

Astydamia latifolia   small, succulent-leaved herbaceous plant with umbels of yellow flowers; grows on salt flats but not common.

Bupleurum handiense   small shrub with glaucous leaves and umbels of small yellow flowers; Riscos de Famara; rare.

Caralluma burchadii   succulent milkweed with four-angled stems growing to 10–15 cm; fruits can be 10 cm. long; north of the island; rare.

Convulvulus caput-medusae   dwarf cushion of a plant with narrow greyish leaves on stems which end in spines; small white flowers; rare on the coasts; locally known as '*chaparro*'.

Convulvulus floridus   bindweed, or '*guaydil*'; grows as a tall plant with small white or pale pink flowers; locally common, especially near euphorbias.

Crepis canariensis perennial herb, having small yellow florets; quite common in the northern part of the island.

Echium lancerottense member of the viper's bugloss family; locally abundant on the Famara massif and in the Haría region.

Erucastrum canariense member of the mustard family, with yellow flowers and large serrated leaves; Haría, Famara massif, La Caleta.

Euphorbia balsamifera the pale green spurge which can sometimes be seen relieving the blackness of volcanic slopes; known locally as '*tabaiba dulce*'.

Euphorbia canariensis the tall 'cactus' known as '*cardón*', which is really a tall succulent shrub; often seen cultivated, but fairly rare in the wild.

Euphorbia obtusifolia greenish-yellow flowered spurge, known as '*tabaiba*' and widespread on low ground.

Euphorbia paralias resembles a fleshy plantain; common on dunes.

Ferula lancerottensis species of giant fennel; locally plentiful in the Haría region and on the massif of Famara; the Spanish name for it is '*canaheja*'.

Frankenia laevis sea heather; mauve flowers from a dense green mat; coastal.

Fumaria praetermissa pink poppy with black-tipped petals; Yaiza, Haría, Arrecife.

Helianthemum thymiphyllum dwarf version of the usual yellow Helianthemum; only on Famara cliffs, 400–600 m.

Helichrysum gossypium tall rock plant with papery white and brown flowers; Riscos de Famara, Montaña de los Helechos; rare.

Hypericum grandiflorum the true St John's wort; grows up to 1 m. high with golden flowers of up to 4.5 cm in diameter; in Lanzarote it is known as '*malfurada*'.

Kickxia heterophylla horn-shaped yellow flower on a small rambling shrub; locally abundant at Arrieta, Playa de Famara, Haría.

Launaea arborescens the low-growing spiny furze bush with tiny yellow florets which is fed to the flames of the volcano at Islote de Hilario; known as '*aulaga*', it occurs widely in the very dry parts of the island.

Lavandula minutolii 'cut-leaved' lavender, known as *mato risco*; thrives in hot dry soil.

Limonium bourgaeii small rock plant known as '*sisempreviva*'; has rosettes of light green leaves and long-stemmed clusters of purple flowers; on cliffs above Playa de Famara and on the Famara massif.

Limonium puberulum similar to the above, but much smaller; found on the cliffs above El Río at 500–600 m.

Lobularia intermedia plant of the mustard family, with greyish-white leaves and small white flowers; locally common on dry rocks.

Lotus glinoides dwarf annual with pinkish-purple flowers of the pea variety; common on sand dunes and by beaches.

Lotus lancerottensis prostrate perennial with flowers like those of yellow broom; common on the coast.

Mesembryanthemum crystallinum ice plant; flowers resemble hoar frost on flat, fleshy leaves; known as *barrilla*, and once used for soap and glass-making.

Mesembryanthemum nodiflorum small white daisy-like flowers and red fleshy leaves.

Minuartia platyphylla pink carnation found up to 700 m.; Riscos de Famara.

Monanthes laxiflora houseleek with grey leaves and yellow or purple flowers; northern areas.

Myrica faya evergreen aromatic shrub with small dark red fruit; Peñas de Chache; very rare.

Ononis hebecarpa small annual with leguminous yellow flowers; locally abundant on Famara massif.

Pancratium canariensis bulbous plant with strap-like leaves and clusters of fragrant flowers like daffodils; occurs near Arrecife, in the Haría region and on Peñas de Chache.

Papaver rhoeas scarlet poppy, general.

Phoenix canariensis the Canary Palm, whose huge leaves grow directly from the trunk; the berries are pale orange and borne in bunches; its natural habitat on Lanzarote is Haría but it has been planted widely; a grove of young palms flourishes beside the road 3 km. S.W. of Teguise.

Plantago famarae very localized large plantain, peculiar to the Riscos de Famara.

Polycarpea divaricata low shrubs with clusters of greenish flowers, common by roadsides, especially near the sea.

Pulicaria canariensis woolly-leaved plant growing in clumps, with abundant golden yellow daisy-like flowers; Famara massif, Montaña de los Helechos; rare.

Ranunculus cortusifolius the indigenous buttercup; Famara massif and Haría.

Reichardia famarae small rock plant only occurring, and that rarely, on the cliffs of Famara; a single flowerhead (yellow) stems from a basal rosette.

Reseda crystallina   mignonette with gold flowers and seed capsules on the stem; Famara massif, Haría, Playa de Famara.

Romulae columnae   small purple iris with a yellow throat; found on low-lying ground.

Rubia fruticosa   rambling prickly succulent, known as '*tasaigo*', with pale yellow flowers in terminal clusters and black berries; Haría, Cueva de los Verdes.

Scilla haemorrhoidalis   short-stemmed purple squill found at the Ermita de las Nieves and near Teguise.

Scilla latifolia   large bulbous plant with purplish-blue flowers on long stalks; it originates in Morocco and is rare on Lanzarote, only occurring in the Famara region.

Sedum lancerottense   unique species named by the English botanist the Rev. R.P. Murray; creeping habit, light green leaves, tiny yellow flowers; Riscos de Famara, Haría, at 400–700 m.

Senecio kleinia   succulent shrub with fleshy leaves and pale yellow florets; often grows in euphorbia colonies; known as '*verode*'.

Tamarix africana   a tamarisk; large shrub or small tree bearing racemes of pale pink or white flowers; locally frequent.

Tamarix canariensis   pink-flowered and more common on Lanzarote than *T. africana*; known locally as '*tarajal*'.

Thymus origanoides   the only wild thyme in the Canary Islands; found on the Famara massif, the Riscos de Famara and around Haría.

Traganum moquinii   small shrub with yellow-green leaves found on sand dunes; Playa de Famara, La Graciosa.

Withania aristata   shrub with laurel-like leaves and black berries; found in low-lying areas; known as '*orobal*'.

Zygophyllum fontanesii   strange succulent shrub with yellowish leaves and white fruit; La Caleta, Arrecife, La Graciosa.

Animals

Until recently, it was generally believed that there were no indigenous mammals at all on Lanzarote. Now, however, a single example has been discovered: a shrew (*Crocidura canariensis*), which scientists believe to be unique to Lanzarote and Fuerteventura. Rabbits were introduced to all the

Dromedaries browsing, Playa Quemada

Canary Islands in the fourteenth and fifteenth centuries, but understandably they are not seen in large numbers on Lanzarote as most of the terrain is so unsuitable. Curiously, the locals insist that rabbits feed on the lichen which tints the black lava in the Timanfaya National Park, but there is little evidence to support the claim. The story may have its origins in history: before 1730 the Timanfaya area was green and fertile and may then have had a thriving rabbit population. Certainly, since Lanzarote people are known familiarly as '*conejeros*' (rabbit hunters), it seems likely that rabbits have been common on the island at some stage.

Hedgehogs can also be found on the island; although originally introduced, they have evolved to be lighter in colour than the western Mediterranean and Moroccan species from which they derive. On Lanzarote and Fuerteventura the species is known as *Erinaceus algirus caniculus.*

The monk seal used to be common on Isla de Lobos, breeding there every year and giving the islet its name; but the European slavers, conquerors and settlers hunted it to extinction. It is now an occasional visitor to Lanzarote, straying from the West African coast. Dolphins and whales are most likely to be seen in warm calm weather.

The camel is, of course, another introduced mammal: the first examples were probably brought over by Agustín de Herrera after his African expedition in 1478. Dromedaries (as they properly are, despite being invariably referred to as '*camellos*' on Lanzarote) play an important role in island life. Besides carrying tourists up the sides of the Fire Mountains, they can even now occasionally be seen drawing a plough in the fields, and this was once a common sight. Sometimes they can be spotted bizarrely harnessed with a donkey: it appears that, as with some racehorses, the humble ass is compatible with and, in some way, comforting to the dromedary, and even if not actually worked together the two animals will often be seen grazing close to each other.

As well as working in agriculture, the camels were widely used as general beasts of burden in earlier times; the salt industry, for instance, used them almost exclusively for transferring its product from the salt-pans to Arrecife. Camels can eat many of the thornier forms of plant life on the island with apparent relish, and appear to mind kneeling on the rough cinders of the *malpaís* not at all. Disease has ended their importation from North Africa, and dromedaries are now bred at Uga, home to almost 300 of them: usually born in March, they start work aged three and live for about 25 years.

Reptiles

There are no snakes on Lanzarote, but there are lizards: one, found around the Jameos del Agua region and known as the Haría lizard (*Gallotia atlantica*) is of such ancient origin that it is believed to be the predecessor of the common lizard. The Mauretanian gecko and the skink may both be seen on the island, and the loggerhead turtle (*Caretta caretta*) frequents the coast but does not nest here.

Birds

Lanzarote lies on one of the major migratory routes between the Americas and northern Europe; thus, although there are some thirty species of birds actually resident, the island is of most interest to birdwatchers as a stopping place for migrants.

Some of the commonest birds are immediately recognisable: the Spanish sparrow, kestrel, linnet, rock dove, raven and herring gull are all familiar to visitors from other parts of Europe. Less easily recognised is **Berthelot's pipit**, which resembles a very small thrush and tends to feed alongside the colourful **trumpeter bullfinch**. This handsome bird, from the African mainland, is the size of a linnet;

it frequents the Timanfaya area where it can be seen picking the seeds out of camel dung after the animals have been fed on maize. Also from North Africa are the **Barbary partridge** (which favours the north of the island and especially the agricultural areas), and the **Egyptian vulture**. The grey, black and white bird often seen on telegraph wires or high bushes is the **great grey shrike**, otherwise known as the 'butcher bird' from its habit of impaling its prey (lizards and beetles) on thorns for later consumption. The **spectacled warbler** is as tame as a British robin and similarly prefers domestic gardens. A **chiffchaff**, peculiar to the Canaries, is distinguished by a rather more warbling song than the common variety (possibly because the absence from Lanzarote of the willow warbler has led to a breakdown in the quality of the chiffchaff's music).

Lanzarote is the home of the only tit in the Canary Islands – a blue tit with a dark head. A strain of the **Houbara bustard**, indigenous to Lanzarote, La Graciosa and Fuerteventura, is becoming re-established, having almost died out: four birds have recently been successfully bred in captivity. In the sandy Papagayo area you may see a **cream-coloured courser**, a handsome bird of the plover family originating in the Sahara and totally at home in a desert environment. On the coast, the majestic **osprey** dives for fish; in the northern waters the coal-black **Bulwer's petrel** nests on the islets and flocks of **Cory's shearwater** colonise Montaña Clara and Alegranza. These exclusively pelagic birds have been protected since 1988; before that they were slaughtered in great numbers for the table in both Lanzarote and La Graciosa. In Arrecife's sea front park, sixty pairs of **cattle egrets** nest in trees near the post office.

In the Tertiary Age, when (it is generally believed) the Canaries were joined to Africa in the form of a great cape, ostriches and elephant birds are known to have arrived from far away Madagascar. Evidence of this was found in 1972 by a group of American geologists who discovered fossilized eggs of the flightless *Aepyornis* (elephant bird) on the island.

Insects

If your holiday is in early spring, after a relatively wet winter, you will not fail to notice the multitude of butterflies on Lanzarote. Swarms of Painted Ladies fill the air, flying around the mountains, across roads, along the beaches and against the plate glass windows of the Castillo San José. The island supports such a large population of these beautiful creatures after a period of rains that the late lepidopterist Denis Owen was able to count forty caterpillars in a square metre in February 1988. The larvae tend to cling to clumps of *Lavatera* (mallow) which, since its introduction from mainland Spain, grows fairly widely. These Painted Ladies do not linger on the island after reaching maturity, but fly north to Europe and as far as Iceland, arriving in the UK during the month of May. Clouded Yellow butterflies are also frequently seen on Lanzarote, as is the Common Blue, which usually feeds on clumps of the yellow-flowered *Lotus lancerottensis*. The Silver Y moth is another noticeable species; interestingly, it usually flies north alongside the Painted Ladies. There are many other less showy insects on the island, including mosquitoes, which can be troublesome in the damper seasons after rain.

Fish

The richest fishing grounds in the whole of the Canaries lie between Lanzarote and the African coast. It is therefore on the eastern side of the island that most of the fish occur. They include *vieja*, *rubio* (flying fish), *cherne* (stone bass), *lenguado* (sole), *caballa* (Atlantic mackerel), *sama* (red sea bream), *dorada* (gold bream), sardines, *bacalao* (cod), *mero* (grouper), *merluza* (hake) and *corvina* (sea bass).

There are of course sea anemones and other creatures which live in rock pools and, most notably, a minute crab can be seen in the waters of Jameos del Agua which is authentically an animal of the deep sea. This is the blind albino *Munidopsis polymorpha*, which was stranded there by the prehistoric eruption of Monte Corona.

HISTORY

The Guanches

The earliest inhabitants of Lanzarote and the other Canary Islands were a race known as the 'Guanches', a name apparently meaning 'men of Tenerife' in their own language ('guan' = 'man', 'Achineh' = Tenerife). They were a fair-skinned people of medium height, with a similar physique to that of the Cro-Magnon skeletons found in the Dordogne in France. It is known that Cro-Magnon tribes found their way to North Africa, and it seems probable that the Guanches were related to the Berber peoples of that region. From archaeological evidence we know they were essentially nomadic; also industrious, using stone weapons and tools and keeping sheep and goats. Besides meat, fish and fruit, a staple of their diet was the *gofio* balls which are still eaten in the islands today – rolled dumplings made of toasted maize or barley: clearly, therefore, some agriculture was practised. They made simple pottery (though they had no wheel), tanned hides and carved wood with flint and basalt tools; horn and bone were also used for manufacturing essential items.

The Guanches often embalmed their dead (though less often, it seems, on Fuerteventura and Lanzarote than on the western islands) and buried them under massive stones, as was the custom over large areas of North Africa in pre-Roman times; they worshipped the sun, moon and stars and believed in an afterlife. The men wore only a knee-length cloak and had long hair cut straight across the forehead. The Lanzarote Guanches were apparently polyandrous, with each woman having about three husbands – we are also told that, being unable to produce milk, they fed their infants with their mouths, and had greatly enlarged lower lips in consequence! Society was divided into castes and the people were usually ruled by a king. A single Guanche language was spoken on all the Canary Islands, with local differences of dialect: it appears to have been most closely related to the Berber language, which originated in ancient Libya, but scholars have claimed to have identified influences as diverse as Greek, Persian, Egyptian and Celtic in it.

These first inhabitants called their island 'Tite-Roy-Gatra' ('Rose-Coloured Hill'). They lived in caves in the lava or in dwellings of the pit type, but they also built simple houses of large stones; these tended to be oval in shape, with the interior living space arranged in the form of a cross.

Oddly, no trace of anything resembling a boat has been found by the archaeologists, and it seems that the Guanches were not great seafarers: fish-bones found in pre-conquest deposits are only of inshore varieties, and there appears to have been little contact between the various islands of the Canary archipelago. From this historians have inferred that the Guanches arrived on boats that were not their own, and an intriguing explanation of their presence is that they were rebellious factions deported by the Romans to the archipe-

Los Hervideros

lago from the province of Mauretania. This theory would make the Canary Islands the first lands in history to be settled by deported convicts.

The origins of the Guanches and the date of their arrival remain controversial topics, but the fact that all the Canaries had genetically similar populations and common cultural traditions is strange, given the lack of inter-island communication, and lends strong support to the deportation theory; so does the fact that the earliest recorded expedition to the island, that of Juba II, the king of the Roman province of Mauretania, reported them uninhabited. The practice of polyandry on Lanzarote may be evidence for the theory also: the original groups of deportees were probably quite small, perhaps only a few dozen per island, and, as in any group of convicts, it is likely that women were at first in short supply.

Today the Guanche culture has completely disappeared and the language survives only in place names. The people have, however, remained; as recently as the end of the last century, apparently, herdsmen could be seen dressed in garments similar to those worn by their indigenous ancestors; and Guanche characteristics can be discerned in the features of many present-day inhabitants, particularly in the more remote regions where the stock is purer: these include broad, short faces, prominent cheekbones, small concave noses and deep-set eyes, often sloping slightly upwards.

Early Visitors

The classical world associated the Canaries with the Fortunate Islands, the mythical home of dead heroes. They were, in fact, probably first discovered by the Carthaginians. As mentioned already, the client king of Mauretania, Juba II, is known to have explored them around the time of Christ: at that time, if Juba's account is to be believed, they were uninhabited, though traces of previous habitation were found (shipwrecked mariners, perhaps?). Ptolemy, the second-century geographer and mathematician, based his influential map on a meridian extending through the Canaries, taking them as the extreme western edge of the known world. Lanzarote and Fuerteventura are mentioned by the Elder Pliny in the first century AD: he referred to them as the 'Purpurariae', an allusion to the purple dye the islands produced from the lichen *orchilla* which grew on the rocks. The earliest artefacts found on Lanzarote which can be dated with any certainty are Roman amphorae of the 2nd-3rd century AD, which have been brought up from shallow water off the coast.

After the Romans the Canary Islands sank back into obscurity for nearly a thousand years. Early Arab navigators naturally came, having first discovered the archipelago around 1016 AD (they called it 'Kaledat'); but it seems not to have been until the fourteenth century that Lanzarote began to be seriously influenced by the outside world. The development of maps, the quadrant and compass and, above all, the invention of the rudder in Europe encouraged maritime exploration. The Castilians and Genoese were in the forefront, and in 1312 (or possibly 1320) a navigator from Genoa, one Lancelotto Malocello, arrived on Lanzarote: he is generally agreed to be responsible for the island's present name. Certainly an atlas made in Mallorca in the year 1339 refers to it as 'Insula de Lanzarotus Marocelus' and depicts the Genoese arms alongside.

Malocello, a vassal of the King of Portugal, is thought to have lived on Lanzarote for several years, being eventually killed by the islanders. The king of the island at that time was Zonzamas, the ruins of whose stronghold can still be seen on Lanzarote, midway between Teguise and Arrecife. Zonzamas and his queen Fayna were succeeded by her daughter (fathered by a visiting Spanish mariner), Ico, and her husband Guanarame. After Guanarame was killed in battle, Ico claimed the throne for their son Guadarfía, destined to be the last Guanche king of Lanzarote.

Through Malocello and other visitors, the existence of the Canary Islands and their potential wealth was brought to European attention: in 1385 a fleet under the command of a noble of Seville, Fernando Peraza, landed on Lanzarote and sacked the island, taking many of the islanders away as slaves, and a second similar expedition followed eight years later.

The French Conquest

Lanzarote's modern history began in 1402, with the arrival of the Normans Gadifer de la Salle (1355–c.1422), a military adventurer from Poitou, and Jean de Bethencourt (1362–1425), a courtier from the Caux region. Popular accounts of Lanzarotean history always credit de Bethencourt with being the conqueror of the island, but this doubtful distinction is in fact more properly due to de la Salle. He owned the ship in which the expedition arrived at Lanzarote and played the more important part in the conquest, only to be ousted later by de Bethencourt, whose descendants then rewrote history to emphasize their ancestor's role at the expense of de la Salle's. An account by de la Salle's priest Boutier survives, however, which gives a truer picture of the expedition. In general the story of the conquest of the Canaries is a depressing one, in which the islanders were usually trusting and humane, while the invaders were a cynical and violent rabble disguising greed under the cloak of Christianity – a contrast which even some of the Europeans involved could not forbear to remark.

The two Frenchmen set sail from La Rochelle on 1 May 1402 with 280 men, a quarrelsome crew many of whom stayed on in Cádiz when the fleet got there; as a result the invading force consisted of only 63 men by the time it reached El Río in July. On arrival, de la Salle had to reconnoitre the island twice before he encountered any inhabitants – doubtless they were all hiding in the caves. However, the Guanches, led by their '*Mencey*', Guadarfía, seem not to have found the newcomers threatening; they appeared willing to welcome the French expedition as a defence against the pirate raids to which the island was constantly subject. De la Salle and de Bethencourt responded to this by immediately embarking on the construction of the Castillo del Rubicón. Ruins of this structure have been found buried in the sand: it was about 1 km from the now abandoned hamlet of Papagayo and 3 km west of the present Castillo de las Coloradas (or Torre del Águila) in the south of the island.

Shortly afterwards, however, the two Frenchmen agreed that, while de la Salle consolidated the conquest, de Bethencourt should return to Europe, there to offer the sovereignty of the island to whichever throne offered the best terms. The latter therefore sailed away, to spend almost two years at the Castilian court, acquiring the personal title of 'Lord of the Islands' in exchange for a promise that the Canaries' ultimate sovereign would be the crown of Castile. During his absence a series of revolts broke out against de la Salle and eventually a full-scale war with the islanders ensued. Lanzarote was finally subdued on 27 February 1404, on which date Guadarfía was baptized and de

Bethencourt, having returned to oust de la Salle, officially became king of Lanzarote. He then set about the conquest of Fuerteventura, aided by Guadarfía and a troop of Lanzaroteños. Hierro and part of Gomera fell not long after, but de Bethencourt soon departed again, for Normandy, whence he returned with 200 French settlers in May 1405. Later the same year he left again, this time for good, leaving his nephew Maciot as viceroy. Shortly after this the first bishop of the Canaries arrived and the first churches were built on the island.

Maciot established Teguise as the capital of the island, naming it after a daughter of King Guadarfía whom he married. Lanzarote then became the base from which the rest of the archipelago was finally subdued, though this took many years to achieve: Tenerife, the last island to capitulate, did not become Spanish until 1496.

Maciot was a cruel and grasping ruler; after a few years he attempted to sell the islands to Portugal and had to be deposed by an expedition from the Spanish mainland. From then on a series of noblemen ruled the islands as feudal lords, of whom the most celebrated was Diego de Herrera. He and his descendants ruled for most of the fifteenth century, resisting further incursions by the Portuguese until, in 1479, the Treaty of Alcaçovas officially recognized that the Canaries were Spanish.

Diego's grandson, Agustín de Herrera y Rochas, was the first Conde (Count) of Lanzarote. He successfully invaded

Teguise

Madeira, and raided the Barbary coast some fourteen times, raising the flag of Castile on African soil in 1478 (and, probably, importing the first dromedaries to the island). Unfortunately, Agustín's aggression seems to have provoked an escalation in the pirate raids by which Lanzarote was ceaselessly troubled. Slave-taking had plagued all the Canaries throughout the fifteenth century (despite a Papal Bull against it having been obtained by the Franciscan missionary Juan de Baeza in 1442), and it continued into the sixteenth and seventeenth: in 1569 the infamous corsair Arals Calafat sacked Teguise and took over 100 slaves. In 1586 the Algerian pirate Amurath took the fortress on Guanapay and burnt Teguise again, taking 200 captives – it was in this raid that all the island's public archives were destroyed, whence the paucity of information about Lanzarotean history. In 1618 Teguise fell yet again to Algerian raiders: the inhabitants took refuge in the Cueva de los Verdes, but nearly a thousand were nevertheless taken away to be sold into slavery. Other pirates who made forays against Lanzarote included the Frenchmen Jean Florin and François LeClerc (known as 'Peg Leg') and the British buccaneers, Sir John Hawkins, John Poole and Sir Walter Raleigh (in 1617).

By the time of the conquest, the population of Lanzarote had probably been reduced to not much more than 300 by slaving forays. At least fifty were killed during the years when the conquest was being consolidated, eighty imprisoned and many of the rest shipped to Europe. In the following 350 years the number of inhabitants increased to some twelve thousand. Throughout these centuries, however, the pattern of settlement seems to have remained fairly static: the islanders, much as today, lived in about fifty villages – though constant raiding from the sea meant that the inland settlements tended to be more populous and important.

Three fortresses, Santa Bárbara on Guanapay overlooking Teguise, the Castillo de San Gabriel protecting Arrecife and the Tower of San Marcial del Rubicón begun by de Bethencourt, provided the island's main defences. In 1596 Philip II commissioned the Italian engineer Leonardo Torriani to strengthen and augment the fortresses of Santa Bárbara and San Gabriel, and they were rebuilt in the form in which we see them today. Torriani wrote an interesting book about the Canaries. Discussing La Graciosa, he

View of Teguise

mentions that English and French privateers would regularly pause there on their way to the Americas, and used it as a base for attacking other shipping, usually local vessels linking the islands with mainland Spain. Occasionally, the Lanzaroteños would retaliate by lying in wait on La Graciosa and falling on the crews of such ships when they again put in there, laden with plunder, on the homeward journey.

By 1600 visitors to the Canaries commonly referred to the Guanches as extinct. As Lanzarote entered the nineteenth century, piratical invasions had become less of a problem and trade and fishing were growing in economic importance; so the predominance of the inland settlements declined, a process which was officially recognized when Arrecife replaced Teguise as the capital in 1852.

The Great Eruptions

Undoubtedly the single most dramatic event in the history of Lanzarote occurred on the night of 1 September 1730, when the Timanfaya volcano erupted, covering some 200 square km of the most fertile part of the island in ash and lava. During the six years of continuous eruption which followed, ten villages were totally destroyed; and in the area to the west of the volcano a column of steam and boulders shooting up from the sea came to rest on land and so altered the configuration of the island in the most dramatic fashion. (The noise of this cataclysm is said to have been audible on Tenerife, 160 miles away.) Many of the islanders fled to

Camels at Timanfaya National Park

The *malpais* at Timanfaya

Jameos del Agua

Storm brewing over Güime

Fuerteventura, others relocated in the north of the island, founding the village of Los Valles. In 1824 a second eruption took place at Tinguatón a little to the north of the Timanfaya area; the effects were less devastating this time, since most of the land affected had already been reduced to a desert of clinker by the events of a century before.

During the nineteenth century emigration was a major factor in Lanzarotean life, reducing the population by over a third. However, the island's capacity to support its people was dramatically increased by the discovery of the *enarenado* system of agriculture (using sand or lava granules to conserve water and feed it to the crops), and by the end of the century the population had stabilized and begun once again to grow.

Modern Times

The Constitution of Cádiz in 1812 gave the Canary Islands the status of a Spanish province for the first time (with Santa Cruz de Tenerife as the capital); it also abolished the feudal system of land-holding, which was still in operation until that date. In 1852 another significant piece of legislation, the Law of Free Ports, granted the Islands the immunity from excise duties which, in modified form, they still enjoy. In 1927 the archipelago was divided into two provinces, and Lanzarote became part of the province of Las Palmas de Gran Canaria. Each island, however, still retains its own governing body, the Cabildo.

The Spanish Civil War brought hardship to Lanzarote. There were no hostilities on the island itself, but extreme demands were made of its meagre agricultural resources, and the situation was aggravated by World War Two, when interruptions in the supply of fuel and other essentials from mainland Spain caused further deprivation. Since that time the most significant changes in the Canary Islands' situation have mainly been due to their discovery by international tourism. Lanzarote was a late starter: as recently as 1970 a mere 25,000 holidaymakers visited the island – today the figure is well over sixty times that number.

The Future

Today Lanzarote is home to some 80,000 people, over half of them residents of Arrecife and the rest distributed between the other six municipalities on the island: Haría, San Bartolomé, Teguise, Tías, Tinajo and Yaiza.

Tourism has already outstripped César Manrique's wildest imaginings, but it is largely thanks to his influence that nevertheless it still affects barely ten per cent of the island. A recent study of the impact of tourism on the environment and the islanders' lifestyle forecast that if all the building projects already approved were to go ahead the number of tourist beds on the island would mushroom from the then existing 36,000 to 250,000 within a very few years, and recommended that future growth should be forcibly limited. An Insular Plan for Lanzarote has therefore been agreed, which permits the number of tourist beds to reach 80,000 by the year 2002; the situation will then be reviewed. The municipalities most affected (Tías, which includes Puerto del Carmen, Yaiza, responsible for Playa Blanca, and Teguise) are to be permitted to add tourist capacity by a set maximum during the next five years. In Tías the present 28,000 beds are not to increase beyond 30,000: Yaiza is to be allowed a dramatic threefold growth to 20,000 and Costa Teguise can grow to a similar level from its present 13,700.

Anyone who loves Lanzarote (or who has experienced the traffic on some of the busier stretches of its roads) must welcome the Cabildo's far-sighted decision, entailing as it does some financial loss due to the need to abandon already existing building contracts. Nevertheless, even with the proposed limitations on growth, the number of tourists on Lanzarote already exceeds the number of indigenous inhabitants. As so often in our modern world, the very factors – heat, aridity, bizarre landscape features – that have kept generations of islanders on the verge of starvation have today become the source of a new and unprecedented prosperity.

Economy and Industry

The economy of Lanzarote has traditionally been based on agriculture and fishing. Despite wind, drought and a shortage of soil, almost all parts of the island, except for the *malpaís* itself, are successfully farmed: onions are a major crop and these, together with tomatoes and potatoes, are grown in sufficient quantities for them to be exported, as is the wine from the local *malvasía* grapes. Other crops include beans, peas, maize, chickpeas, melons, lentils and tobacco.

Agriculture at La Geria

Lanzarote imports six hundred tonnes of bananas each year at present: in an attempt to establish its own crop, six thousand trees have been planted between Sóo and the coast: the first harvest was in autumn 1996. There are no sheep or cows on Lanzarote, but plenty of goats are kept, also donkeys and dromedaries.

The chief characteristic of Lanzarotean agriculture is the *enarenado* process: basically, covering the soil in which crops are to grow with a layer 10–15 cm thick of sand, or more often the black lava granules known as *picón*, in order to prevent the evaporation of moisture through the action of sun and wind and to trap what liquid there is in the atmosphere through absorption by this porous covering. Both soil and lava granules are laboriously replaced every ten years. This process may be natural in origin but has been brought to a peak of sophistication by the Lanzarote farmer in his struggle to live off his blighted land. Statistics show that following the introduction of the *enarenado* process, the population of the island increased quite dramatically after years of decline.

Fishing is a source of employment all around the island. Arrecife, with a fleet of some four hundred boats, is the second biggest port in the Canaries. The city lies close to rich fishing grounds between Lanzarote and the North African coast. It is the major port in Spain for sardines, and cod, grouper, bass, shellfish and *vieja* are also caught in quantity.

Industry, apart from construction, of course, which thanks to the tourist boom is a growth industry, is mostly connected with fishing: five per cent of the workforce are fishermen or are employed in the sardine canning factory in Arrecife. The sardine catch remains the largest in Spain and Lanzarote's tuna fleet also makes an important contribution to the island's economy through exports to Japan. Fish meal for animal feed and fish scales (used in the manufacture of artificial pearls) are also exported. In the past fifteen years, however, tourism has outstripped all the traditional industries and 92 per cent of the island's working population now depend on it directly or indirectly.

SALT

The salt industry, established in the nineteenth century, made a vital contribution to Lanzarote's economy until about forty years ago, but has now practically disappeared. Before the advent of refrigeration, salt was in great demand as a means of preserving the catch when the fishing fleet was at sea for months at a time. The largest shipping enterprise in the Canaries, Naviera Armas, was founded on salt: its first ships supplied the commodity to the trawlers off the Moroccan coast.

To the west of Yaiza, the single remaining area of salt-pans, Las Salinas de Janubio, extends over 480,000 square metres. Currently producing only a small yield of brine (used in the canning industry), the chequerboard pattern of the old salt-pans, the whiteness of the drying heaps of salt and the turquoise of the shallow lagoon make an unusual and much photographed sight from the old Yaiza to Playa

The salt-pans at Janubio

Blanca road. In 1991 this area was declared a National Heritage site, and plans to restore the structure of the salt-pans and the windmills which powered the plant were drawn up in 1993. A salt museum and cultural centre will also be built. The Salinas del Río, opposite La Graciosa and visible from the Mirador del Río, are no longer in use: like Janubio these salt-pans constitute an important birdwatching area.

Until the advent of tourism, when their valuable sites were bought by developers, there were large *salinas* at Matagorda, north of Puerto del Carmen, and at Costa Teguise, where the name of the 5-star luxury Meliá Salinas hotel is their only memorial.

Traditionally the people of Lanzarote have greatly appreciated their heritage of salt, and this is shown most clearly in Arrecife at Corpus Christi. Whereas in many Spanish towns, carpets of flowers are laid in the streets on this day, around the church of San Ginés the ground is covered with salt dyed in vivid colours and laid out in dazzling patterns. This is to demonstrate the people's gratitude to God for their gift of salt despite the shortage of fresh water, and hence flowers, on their island. Sadly, the salt for these *fiestas* has nowadays to be imported.

The water used for drinking and all other purposes on Lanzarote is produced from salt water by modern desalination plants.

COCHINEAL

One of Lanzarote's more unusual traditional industries is the farming of the cochineal beetle (*Coccus cacti*), which centres on Mala, Guatiza and that part of the north-east coast. Here the landscape consists of field after field of prickly pear (*Opuntia ficus-indica*), known locally as *tunera*, which is cultivated as a host for the cochineal beetle which feeds parasitically on its flesh. Native to Mexico, the beetle is covered with white down, which since the cacti tend to be shrouded in enormous cobwebs, makes it difficult to see. Farming involves distributing the beetles over the cacti, ensuring that each plant has its share of productive females, and harvesting the larvae after three months, These are removed from the plants with a spatula, killed in hot water, dried in the sun and crushed to a powder which produces the red dye. Cochineal is used in cosmetics, food processing,

A windmill at Guatiza

pharmaceutical products, and some soft drinks and aperitifs. Nowadays synthetic dyes have tended to usurp its role, but there is still a market for non-toxic 'natural' colourings as the fields in this part of Lanzarote testify. It takes about 140,000 insects to produce 1 kg. of cochineal and the yield is processed near Teguise.

CULTURE AND FOLKLORE

César Manrique

The tragic death of César Manrique in September 1992 deprived Lanzarote of its most celebrated inhabitant and foremost champion. His works as architect, abstract artist and sculptor are to be found worldwide, but his enduring legacy remains in his home island, which has conferred on him the title of '*Hijo Predilecto*' (Favourite Son).

Born in Arrecife on 24 April 1919, Manrique spent his formative years at La Caleta de Famara, where he grew up close to nature and developed a deep feeling for the landscape of his native land. His art often draws on themes and patterns from this landscape: black basalt, white cubic houses, 'Turk's cap' chimneys, vivid flowers and, of course, the sea. Manrique also published *Lanzarote Arquitectura Inédita*, a book of photographs cataloguing all the buildings of the island. His espousal of Lanzarote's cause evolved into a crusade in the 1960s, when he returned to his homeland after four years in New York. The changes in the island horrified him, particularly the multi-storey Gran Hotel in Arrecife, and he brought his considerable powers of persuasion to bear on the Cabildo (the island's governing body) in the cause of protecting what remained of Lanzarote's unique character. Further high-rise building was to be banned absolutely, as were roadside advertising hoardings; indiscriminate rubbish tipping was outlawed, electricity cables and telephone lines were to be laid underground wherever feasible; above all, development was to be zoned and permitted only if it blended with the vernacular style.

Manrique was determined to make Lanzaroteños proud of their heritage and traditional, modest architecture, in direct contact with nature. The cubic forms and white and green livery for all buildings was actively encouraged, producing the harmonious effect that is so noticeable on the island today. He also began a series of works which are today among Lanzarote's major attractions. His first ideas in this direction came to him as he sat at the entrance to Jameos del Agua (at that time foul-smelling and overflowing with

Monumento El Campesino, Mozaga

rubbish) and dreamed of turning the cave into a beauty spot for both Lanzaroteños and visitors to enjoy. His first project to be realised was the Campesino Monument at Mozaga, symbolizing Fertility and the peasant's heroic struggle to wrest a living from his harsh environment. Next, this friendly and unconventional man, who never drew detailed plans and had no formal architectural training, designed and oversaw the building of the restaurant on the Islote de Hilario, enhanced the Cueva de los Verdes, built the Mirador del Río and converted the Castillo de San José into an art gallery and restaurant; in Arrecife itself (a city he professed to find profoundly depressing) he designed the Almacén arts complex and most recently completed the Cactus Garden at Guatiza. Tireless in his mission to enhance his beloved island and beautify it with artistic displays that harmonise with its harsh beauty, he was working on a Wind Museum to complement the large wind-energy plant at Los Valles when he died.

Manrique succeeded triumphantly in rescuing Lanzarote from its position as the 'Cinderella' of the Canaries, and his influence is everywhere to be seen. Impressively, he never received a peseta in payment for his designs, being content with the gratitude of his fellow-islanders. With typical generosity, when Manrique moved to Haría in 1988 he presented the island with his villa, the Taro de Tahiche, a fabulous dwelling built within a series of volcanic bubbles, and surrounded by gardens. Opened to the public six months before his death, it houses a fine collection of contemporary art, including works by himself.

Thanks to Manrique's efforts Lanzarote remains largely free of the worst excesses of development. Nevertheless he professed himself saddened by Puerto del Carmen ('stinking of drains and tomato sauce'), and found the wholesale development of the Costa Teguise particularly depressing: he approved the Meliá Salinas Hotel, but never intended that it should be surrounded by development on the scale seen today, some of which reduces the vernacular style to kitsch or respects local tradition not at all. In 1986, in despair at the uncontrolled growth, he was moved to deliver a manifesto entitled 'Lanzarote is Dying' to the King. In his own words, 'a small island must be like a theatre – when all the seats are taken, then no more tickets can be sold'. Nevertheless, Manrique's achievement has been great, as anyone who has seen the high-rise blocks and garish billboards of Gran Canaria, for example, will appreciate. His countrymen have recovered their pride and thousands of people all over the world appreciate their island, where a strange and unique natural beauty has been preserved for generations to come.

Art Galleries

The 18th-century Castillo de San José overlooking the commercial harbour at Arrecife is home to the International Museum of Contemporary Art. Once known as the 'Starvation Fortress' (because Charles III ordered its construction to provide employment for the indigent islanders), the fort was cleverly converted by César Manrique to house a small recital room and a magnificent restaurant area as well as the gallery, which holds regular special exhibitions and displays an impressive permanent collection (open 11.00–21.00 daily, admission free). Castillo de San José is worth visiting, not least to see the interior of the fort itself. Also in Arrecife there are occasional art exhibitions at the Casa Cultural

Castillo de San José, Arrecife

Agustín de la Hoz (next to the Post Office, tel: 812750), and at the El Aljibe gallery, part of César Manrique's El Almacén complex at 26–33 Calle José Betancourt. Manrique's old studio, opposite El Almacén at no. 26, can also be visited, with a permanent exhibition of his work (open 10.00–13.30 and 17.30–20.30 Mon–Fri). Beside El Charco the Sala Punto de Encuentro shows paintings intermittently throughout the year.

César Manrique's former home at **Tahiche** lies on the right of the San Bartolomé road, near the roundabout surmounted by one of his wind sculptures. Known as the Fundación César Manrique, this unique structure with its collection of modern art – Picasso, Miró and Tàpies are all represented – and innovative architecture is unmissable, and has become the fourth most visited museum in the whole of Spain. It is open Mon–Sat 10.00–19.00, Sundays 10.00–15.00 (admission 800 ptas, children free; tel: 843138, fax: 843463).

In **Puerto del Carmen**, the Espiral art gallery at Montaña Tropical (calle El Toscón) has changing exhibitions, while in **Yaiza**, contemporary paintings and sculpture can be seen at the Galería Yaiza (open 17.00–19.00 Mon–Sat) on the main road through the village, and at the Casa de la Cultura Don Benito Pérez Armas in Plaza de los Remedios (open 16.00–19.00 daily except Sundays and *fiestas*). A permanent exhibition of the works of artist, sculptor and composer Ildefonso Águilar is on view at the Geo gallery, **Puerto Calero**. There are also periodic exhibitions in the Palacio Spínola, Convent of San Francisco and Palacio Museo Marqués Agustín de Herrera y Rojas, all in **Teguise** (all open 10.00–16.30 Mon–Fri, 10.00–15.00 at weekends).

For up to date information about all these galleries, the Culture Department of the island government can be contacted on tel: 800569 (fax: 802656).

Museums

Arrecife's **archaeological museum** is in the Castillo de San Gabriel which guards the seaward approach to the town (open 09.00–14.45 Mon–Fri, admission 100 ptas). It displays Stone Age artcfacts, many of them from the Zonzamas ruins, plans of some of the island's prehistoric sites and a display of primitive pottery fashioned by Juan Brito of Mozaga. An attractive mid-eighteenth-century house on the sea front, **Casa de los Arroyo**, was transformed in 1995 into a museum to commemorate the life and work of the eminent Arrecife-born physicist Blas Cabrera Felipe, who was associated with Einstein and Marie Curie (open 10.30–13.30 and 17.30–20.30 Mon–Fri, admission free). A statue of Blas Cabrera stands in the sea front park, next to the old *parador*.

Lanzarote's third fortress, the Castillo de Santa Bárbara overlooking Teguise, houses the **Museo del Emigrante Canario**, devoted to documents connected with natives of the Canaries who emigrated to the Americas in the nineteenth and early twentieth centuries (open 10.00–16.30 Tues–Fri, 11.00–15.00 weekends, admission 300 ptas, children free).

At Mozaga, the **Casa Museo del Campesino** displays old farm implements and examples of native crafts: a dromedary grinds maize to be turned into *gofio* (see p.16) and served in the adjoining restaurant. In addition to a souvenir shop there is a permanent exhibition of work by Lanzarote's two eminent potters, Doña Dorotea of Muñique and her pupil Juan Brito.

In Tiagua, a few metres along the road to Sóo, a right turn brings you to the **Museo Agrícola El Patio**: this is the expertly restored home of the late Dr José María Barreto (1924–1993), who bought the old farmhouse when it was falling into decay. The farm has become a microcosm of rural Lanzarote, and contains a few animals, working windmills, tableaux, exhibitions and demonstrations of traditional crafts. There is also a small collection of finds from the El Bebedero archaeological site (1st century AD) which lies within the villa. Opening hours are Mon–Fri 10.00–17.00, Sat 10.00–14.30, closed on Sunday (tel: 529106), admission 600 ptas. Next to the church at Haría is a Museum of Sacred Art which contains altarpieces, old paintings etc. (open Mon–Fri 11.00–13.00 and 16.00–18.00); beside the restaurant El Cortijo at the southern end of the village the idiosyncratic Almogarem 'Museum of Miniatures' features such exhibits as a 0.5 sq. cm paper kite made by the Spanish poet Unamuno.

Although Lanzarote is already so well endowed with museums, future plans include an archaeological museum at the Zonzamas ruins, an ecological museum in La Geria and a wind museum at Los Valles.

Music

Concerts are infrequent but worth looking out for, as Lanzarote offers some interesting and unusual venues; there is a recital room within the Castillo San José, a magnificent subterranean auditorium seating 550 people at Jameos del Agua and, most unusual of all, the concert area deep within the Cueva de los Verdes. Recitals are also held in the Casa Cultural Agustín de la Hoz in Arrecife. Publicity for musical events is not good: the Culture Department can provide up to date information (tel: 800569, fax: 802656).

A feature of musical life for the last seven years has been the Visual Music Festival held in October. The brainchild of local artist, sculptor, photographer and composer, Ildefonso Águilar, the festival uses both the cave venues and has also organised a concert in the El Cuervo volcanic crater in the Timanfaya park. Águilar's speciality is 'ambient' music, a genre developed with his friend and collaborator Brian Eno; some of the music heard on the Timanfaya 'Ruta de los Volcanes' and in the Cueva de los Verdes is Águilar's, and the volcanic auditoria make perfect settings for it.

Festivals

Most of Lanzarote's local festivals are concentrated in the summer months. Those associated with a Saint's Day typically commence a week or more before the day itself and feature sporting contests, wrestling matches, displays of folk dancing and singing, fireworks, feasting and general merry-making, culminating in a procession in honour of the saint. The spring and winter are enlivened by the extravagant costumes and elaborate floats of the February Carnival and, at Christmas, by nativity plays and processions all over the island which are based on local traditions of great age and are often the result of months of rehearsal. Some *fiestas* are more spectacular than others. The Mancha Blanca *fiesta* in September is one of the largest: people come, often on foot, to perform a *romería* (pilgrimage), from all over the island, to eat, drink, socialize and view a dramatic representation portraying the Virgin stopping the lava flow as it approaches the village. On the last Saturday of the Fiestas del Carmen (August), a flotilla of fishing boats bearing effigies of the saint and adorned with flowers and palm fronds puts to sea from the harbour in the Old Town of Puerto del Carmen.

Information about specific festivals is available from Tourist Offices; they include

January 5	**Teguise, Arrecife** Cabalgata de Reyes Magos (Epiphany Procession, featuring dromedaries)
February	**Arrecife, Puerto del Carmen, Costa Teguise, Playa Blanca** Carnival
February 3	**Tías** Fiesta de la Candelaria
May 15	**Uga** Fiesta de San Isidro
May 24	**Montaña Blanca, Mala** Fiesta de la María Auxiliadora
Corpus Christi	**Arrecife and elsewhere** Processions, carpets of salt
June 13	**Güime, Los Valles** Fiesta de San Antonio
June 21	**Las Breñas** Fiesta de San Luis Gonzaga
June 24	**Haría** Fiesta de San Juan
June 29	**Mácher, Máguez** Fiesta de San Pedro
July 7	**Femés** San Marcial del Rubicón
July 16	**Arrieta, La Santa, La Graciosa, Playa Blanca, Teguise, Tías** Fiestas de N.S. del Carmen

July 25	**Tahiche** Fiesta de San Felipe Santiago
August 1	**Puerto del Carmen** Fiestas del Carmen (for 2 weeks)
August 25	**Arrecife** Fiesta de San Ginés
September 8	**Yaiza** Fiesta de la Virgen de los Remedios
September 9	**Tiagua** Fiesta de N.S. de Socorro
September 15	**Mancha Blanca** Fiesta de N.S. de los Dolores
September 20	**Guatiza** Fiesta de Cristo de los Aguas
October 7	**Arrecife** Fiesta de la Virgen de la Rosario
October 24	**Teguise** Fiesta de San Rafael
November 30	**Tao** Fiesta de San Andrés
December 4	**Máguez** Fiesta de Santa Bárbara
December 13	**Mozaga** Fiesta de Santa Lucía
December 24	**Teguise and elsewhere** '*Rancho de Pascua*', nativity play, processions

Crafts

A vigorous tradition of craftwork has received useful encouragement from tourism: simple pottery, embroidery, traditional dolls, hats and baskets of palm leaves, wood-carving and jewellery made from olivine, the local precious stone, can all be found in the island's shops and market stalls. The traditional crafts market held on Sunday mornings in Teguise has massively expanded in the last few years and now flows into half the streets in the town (while dwellers on the outskirts transform any suitable space into unofficial car parks and vie for visitors' custom). Other crafts markets take place in the Pueblo Marinero centre, Costa Teguise, on Friday evenings, and on Wednesday mornings at the Punta Limones centre, Playa Blanca. Traditional craftsmen can be seen at work at the Casa Museo del Campesino (p.65), at the Museo Agrícola El Patio (pp.65–6) and at the Taller de Artesanía in Haría, which also has a shop (open 10.00–13.00 and 16.00–18.30 Mon–Fri). During the important September *fiesta* at Mancha Blanca, there is a large crafts fair at which the expertise of all the Canary Islands is on show. Potters whose

The fleamarket at Teguise

studios can be visited include Juan Brito (just west of Mozaga), who makes figures and traditional Guanche artefacts without a wheel, and Doña Dorotea of Muñique, a remarkable nonagenarian who fires primitive pots and small figurines with prominent sexual characteristics in the open air. In Teguise a speciality is the manufacture of the *timple*, the unique 5-stringed ukelele of the Canaries, often made of rosewood (see also p. 101).

Libraries

During July, August and September a mobile Beach Library, with titles in English, German, French and Spanish, parks beside the tourist office on Puerto del Carmen sea front (open daily 10.00–14.00, 16.00–20.00). Also in Puerto del Carmen, new and secondhand books in English can be bought and resold at The Bookswap, calle Timanfaya 4, and SusLibros, calle Teide.

SPORTS AND ACTIVITIES

There is no lack of sporting facilities of every kind on Lanzarote. Dedicated sportsmen and women can, indeed, base their whole holiday around them, by staying at Club La Santa on the north coast near Tinajo, which has unbeatable facilities and a year-round programme. Established on the island in 1983, this highly successful complex regularly plays host to Olympic athletes such as Linford Christie, Colin Jackson and Liz McColgan, and provides winter training for some of Europe's best known football teams. Frank Bruno prepared for his world championship here and Miguel Indurain, four times winner of the Tour de France, has taken part in cycling events. The Ironman Triathlon, a major international event involving swimming, cycling and a marathon, is held in Lanzarote each June under the auspices of the Club, which offers its residents facilities and equipment for over 25 leisure and sporting activities, complete with instruction if required. As well as an athletics stadium, football pitch, 50m swimming pool and ten tennis courts, La Santa has squash and badminton courts, a windsurfing school, fitness centre, and facilities for basketball, handball, softball, volleyball, rugby, aerobics, table tennis, mini-golf, bowls, cycling, orienteering and *boules*. Information on fully inclusive holidays can be obtained in the UK from Club La Santa Ltd, The Grange, 16 St Peter's Street, St Albans, Herts AL1 3NA (tel: 01727 845151, fax: 01727 843535), in Germany from Sperberhorst 11, 22459 Hamburg (tel: 040 5510034) or on Lanzarote from Club La Santa, Tinajo (tel: 840620, fax: 840152).

There is a sports centre in Costa Teguise, Toca Sport in Avda del Jablillo, which offers tennis, squash, five-a-side football and skateboarding, as well as a gymnasium and sauna, swimming pool, yoga, table tennis, etc. (tel: 590617); in Puerto del Carmen the Club Insular in Urb. Playa Blanca next to the Fariones Hotel provides tennis, squash, volleyball, basketball and table tennis (open daily to non-members 09.30–22.00, tel: 825208), while Castellana Sport, Calle Guanapay 2, has a fully equipped gym with instruction, aerobics, bodybuilding and keep fit, squash courts and pool table (Mon–Fri 08.00–22.30, Sats 10.00–21.00, closed Sun; temporary membership 1000 ptas per day, tel: 825493). In Arrecife the World Class Gym, José Antonio 87, opens 07.30–22.30 Mon–Fri, 10.00–14.00 Sats and offers aerobics, gymnastics and martial arts.

CYCLING

Bicycles can be hired at all the main tourist centres for approx. 1000 ptas per day, and mountain bikes may also be hired on the waterfront at La Graciosa. Off road cycling 'safaris' on mountain bikes, often in conjunction with a jeep ride to the venue, are organised by Tommy's Bikes (tel: 592327) and Hot Bike (tel: 590304) in Costa Teguise, Sun Bike in Puerto del Carmen (near the Hotel Los Fariones, tel: 513440) and Club La Santa.

DIVING

The unpolluted waters of the Atlantic offer divers visibilities of 20 metres or more. Several varieties of large fish can be seen, among them barracuda, grouper, conger, tuna and rays; recently an underwater nature reserve, Los Erizos, has been created off the coast near Puerto del Carmen where ten old fishing boats have been sunk to a depth of 30m with the aim of attracting marine life.

Scuba diving schools in Puerto del Carmen, all with tuition in English and German, include Atlántica at the Fariones aparthotel (tel: 510717), R.C. Diving at the Aquarium commercial centre (tel: 514290) and Barracuda Club, Hotel La Geria (Playa de los Pocillos, tel: 512765). At Costa Teguise, Calipso Diving (tel: 590879) and Diving Lanzarote (tel: 590407) operate from Playa de las Cucharas; at Puerto Calero, Catlanza (tel: 513022) offers scuba diving, and Moby Dick (tel: 173240) at Playa Quemada supervises local dives and conducts trips to Lobos and La Graciosa. There is also diving at Club La Santa (see above).

Diving is an expensive sport: one dive may cost 4000 ptas exclusive of the hire of a boat and all equipment, and a beginner's course of six dives may cost approx. 23,000 ptas (including boat and equipment hire). Divers are required to join the Spanish Diving Club (FEDAS), so take two passport photographs and your passport with you; supplementary insurance is also advisable. Arrecife's main hospital is equipped with a decompression chamber. *NB It is dangerous to fly less than 24 hours after diving.*

FISHING

Deep sea fishing expeditions can be arranged from the harbours of Puerto del Carmen, Playa Blanca and Órzola; occasional night trips are advertised, for which reservations need to be made two days in advance. Catlanza in Puerto Calero offer daily excursions on their catamaran, departing at 10.00 and returning at 15.00 (5500 ptas in 1996): sport fishing, bottom fishing and shark fishing are all featured. Spear fishing is only permitted around certain stretches of the coast, basically in the extreme north-east, between the southern edge of Puerto del Carmen and Punta Papagayo and off two stretches of the west coast. Fishing from the rocks is possible at several places around the island, though the seas on the north and west coasts are often too rough.

For fishing trips out of Arrecife, call Nautiboat (513576). A fishing club meets on the first Saturday of each month (tel: 825065 for details).

FLYING

Sightseeing excursions and lessons are offered by Aviador Flying School based at the airport (mobile tel: 908 354193).

GOLF

Lanzarote's only golf course is in the Costa Teguise resort, designed by the late John D. Harris and opened in 1980, the lush fairways of its 18 holes lovingly watered and its bunkers composed of black sand. The overall length is 5853m for men and 5178m for ladies, par for the course is 72 and a handicap of 28 (men) or 32 (ladies) is required. There are two driving ranges, a pitch-and-putt course, and a putting green; all equipment can be hired. Green fees in 1996 were 6000 ptas (2500 junior); further information from Club de Costa Teguise (open 08.00–19.30 daily, tel: 590512, fax: 590490).

KARTING

Lanzarote's karting track, just south of San Bartolomé on the Arrecife road, is open from 10.00 until sunset; it has a bar, cafeteria and children's playground (tel: 512195).

RIDING

'Lanzarote a Caballo' ('Lanzarote on Horseback') is reached up a dirt track by turning right at the km 17 post between Mácher and Uga. The stables are open 10.00–14.00 and 17.00–20.00 (16.00–19.00 in winter) and offer riding lessons (2500 ptas per hour) as well as full- or half-day excursions on horseback to La Geria, Playa Quemada or Playa Blanca via Femés: prices in 1996 were 7000 ptas for a half-day and 10,000 for a full day's ride (tel: 830314). Rancho Texas Equestrian Centre is well signed from the southern end of Playa de los Pocillos beach (calle Noruega) and lies just north of the Puerto del Carmen bypass (although it is not reachable from it). Riding instruction, pony trekking, dressage and jumping are all on offer, and there is self-catering accommodation with a swimming pool (tel: 173247, fax: 175248).

The view south from Femés

SAILING

Puerto Calero is a purpose-built yacht marina, designed by Lanzaroteño Luis Ibañez. With 150 berths the marina has a 24-hour harbourmaster service and a full range of facilities including fuel, a slipway with travel-left bridge, workshops for repairs and painting, shops, a restaurant with a good reputation and an art gallery (tel: 511442). Other harbours where yachts can moor are Órzola, Puerto del Carmen, Playa Blanca and Arrecife, where the sailing club, Casino Club Nautico, is at calle Dr Roberto Negrín 1 (tel: 811850). In summer Arrecife bay is the scene of lateen sailing contests between 5-metre boats with a four-man crew.

SWIMMING

There are beaches all round the coast of Lanzarote, but they vary considerably in safety (and colour). In general those on the south (Playa Blanca, Papagayo) and east coasts (south of Órzola, Arrieta, Costa Teguise, the Arrecife beaches, Playa Honda to Puerto del Carmen, Playa Quemada) offer the best swimming. On the west coast, the sea at Playa de Famara is frequently rough, with a dangerous undertow, though the beach is sandy and spectacular; the black beaches at Playa de Janubio and El Golfo are similarly treacherous. There is a glorious beach on La Graciosa, Playa de las Conchas, reachable after a longish walk or cycle ride across the middle of the island. The enticing beach of Playa del Risco, visible from below the Mirador del Río, is only accessible down a vertiginous cliff path from a point just west of Ye.

Topless bathing is quite common; naturism and nude bathing are largely confined to the smaller Papagayo beaches in the south. Sunbeds and umbrellas can be hired on a few of the town beaches.

TENNIS, SQUASH AND BADMINTON

Virtually all the large hotels and apartment complexes, as well as the sports centres, have courts and hire out equipment; many have floodlighting and employ coaches.

WALKING

Large areas of Lanzarote, particularly in the north, are covered by a maze of tracks, though making progress over the volcanic *malpaís* itself is not very pleasant. The Canarian environmental organisation ICONA conducts two regular walks (free of charge): a volcano walk from the dromedary centre (p.86) at 10.30 on Mon, Tues, Thurs and Fri (3 km, 'easy'), and, on Wednesday at 08.30, a coastal walk from their office at calle La Laguneta 64, Tinajo, which negotiates the twisted lava border of Timanfaya National Park and reaches the sea at Playa de la Madera (9 km, 'difficult'). Both walks are for a maximum of seven people and concentrate on the geology, flora and fauna of the *malpaís* (tel: 840238, fax: 840251). Noel Rochford's *Landscapes of Lanzarote* (Sunflower Books, London, 1994) describes nine walks in detail, including a dramatic scramble down the Riscos de Famara to the beach and salt-pans below the Mirador del Río.

WATERSPORTS

The regular strong, clean winds in the Canaries (often reaching force 4 or 5) have established the archipelago as one of the top centres in the world for **windsurfing**; Lanzarote, with good swells in the north and west (where wave faces can reach 10m in height) and more sheltered coasts in the south, provides opportunities for all levels of skill from novice to world-class board sailor. Conditions change daily, but the Playa de los Pocillos and Matagorda beaches are usually the best for beginners, plus, of course, the manmade lagoon at La Santa. For intermediate windsurfers, Puerto del Carmen, Playa de las Cucharas and Playa del los Charcos (both at Costa Teguise), and Playa Dorada at Playa Blanca are all recommended; while for the more expert, La Santa (offshore) and Playa de Famara can provide an exciting challenge.

Windsurfing schools include: Club La Santa (see above), Lanzarote Surf Company (Playa de las Cucharas, tel/fax: 591974 – the only F2 centre in Lanzarote); Nathalie Simon Windsurfing Club (Playa de las Cucharas) and Nina Navarro Bic Sport at Playa de Matagorda (tel: 510140). All of these also hire out body boards and funboards. Prices for windsurf hire were around 2500 ptas per hour in 1996, or 6500 per day; a 10-hour beginner's course cost 25,000 ptas in 1996 at Lanzarote Surf Company.

Surfing can be enjoyed at Club La Santa (call Pedro on 840279), Playa de Famara (Surf School Lanzarote, tel: 173173), Arrieta and Playa de las Cucharas (Lanzarote Surf Company). Surf boards and boogie boards are available for hire. **Water skiing** is available with Catlanza (tel: 513022) and at Canary Fun (mobile tel: 989 351935), both at Puerto Calero, Puerto del Carmen and Playa Blanca.

Canary Fun rents out Kawasaki 750 **jet skis** from the harbours of Puerto del Carmen, Playa Blanca and Puerto Calero, and also from Hotel San Antonio, Puerto del Carmen: rides are available from 11.00–18.30 daily (1996 prices were 2500 ptas for 15 minutes, 4500 for 30 and 8000 for an hour). Free transport from the Cafe Journal (near the Fariones Hotel) is offered to Puerto Calero or Playa Blanca (mobile tel: 989 351935). Catlanza in Puerto Calero also rent jet skis (tel: 513022). **Pedaloes** can be hired for around 700 ptas per 30 minutes from most beaches which hire out sunbeds and parasols.

The most popular sport among Lanzaroteños, however, is **wrestling** (*lucha Canaria*): there are eight teams on the island and matches draw larger crowds than local football matches. Of extremely ancient origin, possibly Guanche (though similar wrestling is also part of Cuban and Venezuelan culture), the sport is governed by rules and traditions of great complexity, with no fewer than 43 permissible grips. Each member of a team of 12 must confront each of the opposing team in turn, with the aim of forcing him to touch the ground with any part of his body other than his (bare) feet. Wrestling matches are held in a sand-covered ring (*terrero*) and are a regular feature in Arrecife and Tías throughout the year, and elsewhere at *fiesta* time (see local press for details). Displays for tourists can be seen each Tuesday and Wednesday evening at 20.00 at the Timanfaya restaurant in Uga (tel: 830003). Another traditional Canarian sport is **stick fighting** (*juego del palo*), in which two opponents fence with flexible rods.

Excursions

BOAT TRIPS

Boat excursions around the Lanzarote coast, and to the islands of Lobos and Fuerteventura, are run by Blue Delfín (tel: 512323) from the harbour at Puerto del Carmen with free bus transport from Matagorda, Playa de los Pocillos and Costa Teguise. Prices in 1996 were: Papagayo beaches (with long stay), 3000 ptas; Lobos and Fuerteventura (including lunch and *sangría*), 6000 ptas; one-hour mini-cruise, 1500 ptas (children half price in all cases). The boat used is a 250-seat catamaran with 32 underwater windows. There is also a boat service from Playa Blanca to the Papagayo beaches, leaving the harbour at 10.45, 12.00, 13.30 and 15.30 with an hour's stay (1000 ptas).

Well established and very popular is the 'pirate cruise' on the 30-metre schooner *Marea Errota*, which leaves daily from Playa Blanca harbour at 10.00 for the Papagayo beaches and a voyage up the east coast, returning at 16.00. The crew enliven periods at anchor by performing gymnastics in the rigging, and the atmosphere on board is good-humoured and relaxed. (Tickets from agencies or tel: 510269 for information.)

The 'aquascope', a ten-seater mini-submarine, sets out from Puerto del Carmen harbour every half-hour from 10.00 until sunset to visit the nearby Los Erizos underwater marine park. This is a collection of wrecked fishing boats sunk to a depth of 36 metres which attracts a wide variety of fish. The water is clear and the aquascope permits good viewing.

Day excursions by boat can also be made to La Graciosa and Fuerteventura (see below).

COACH TRIPS

As one would expect, there are plenty of opportunities to see Lanzarote by coach if you have not hired a car: almost any travel agent or tour operator will offer a selection. Popular excursions include a full-day trip covering the Fire Mountains (including camel ride), El Golfo, La Geria and Yaiza (expect to pay 5,000–6,000 ptas for this) and half-day tours of the north, taking in Teguise, Haría, Mirador del Río, the

Cueva de los Verdes and Jameos del Agua. There are also opportunities to visit Teguise flea market on Sunday mornings, to sample the evening entertainment at Jameos del Agua, dinner at El Diablo restaurant, Timanfaya, or the wrestling at Uga. Any tour representative or travel agent will organise such excursions for you.

PLEASURE FLIGHTS

Various aerial tours of the island can be made: a flight over La Geria and Timanfaya cost 7900 ptas per person in 1996, Teguise, Famara, Mirador del Río and Haría 9900 ptas, and a tour of the whole island 12,400 ptas (tel: 840100 for information). Lanzarote Skydive Centre (tel: 840114) offers parachute jumps.

FUERTEVENTURA

Regular ferries sail between Playa Blanca and Corralejo in the north of the neighbouring 'tranquil island' of Fuerteventura. Naviera Armas (tel: 811019) sail daily at 09.00, 11.00, 17.00 and 19.00, returning from Corralejo at 08.00, 10.00, 14.00 and 18.00. The single fare in 1996 was 1700 ptas (children 850, students 1200, over-60s 1500). Lineas Fred. Olsen (tel: 517266) depart from Playa Blanca at 08.00, 10.00, 14.00 and 18.00; from Corralejo at 09.00, 11.00, 17.00 and 19.00. Their fares are slightly higher but include a free bus transfer from Puerto del Carmen (at 09.00 or 17.00) and

Church of San Roque, Tinajo

Ermita de Los Nieves

Castillo de Santa Bárbara, Guanapay

(Top left) Uga,   (Middle left) The waterfront at Arrecife,
(Bottom left) Riscos de Famara,   (Above) Caletón Blanco

(Above) The beach at Puerto del Carmen,
(Below) The Papagayo Beaches

back from Playa Blanca (at 09.55 and 17.55). Both companies offer a 'package': a car and three passengers pay around 6000 ptas. The crossing between the islands takes 35 minutes.

Corralejo, the port of arrival, has grown from a tiny and rather poor fishing village into a small holiday town with some very pleasant accommodation for tourists. The town beaches are clean, white and safe for swimming; further round the coast to the south there is an enormous stretch of sand, known as Las Dunas, which is, in conjunction with Isla de Lobos, a nature reserve. There are, however, two large hotels on this beach, built before the nature reserve was created.

Most tour operators and travel agents offer an excursion (typically costing around 6–7000 ptas including lunch) to Fuerteventura, which includes a tour of the northern part of the island; but if you are travelling independently you will have to bring your own car over from Lanzarote or hire one in Corralejo.

Much longer than a day is needed to see Fuerteventura, as it is very large – second in size only to Tenerife among the Canaries. The most sparsely populated island in the archipelago, Fuerteventura is dry, with vast treeless landscapes consisting of extinct volcanoes and miles of deserted sand dunes and beaches. The highest point, in the extreme south, is Pico de Jandía (807 m). The lonely plains and valleys are mainly arid and bare, but near the more important villages some market gardening is contrived: onions, tomatoes, alfalfa and *henequen* (a type of agave used to make rope and twine) are grown, and goats are kept which appear to thrive on practically nothing. This agriculture would seem scarcely enough to support the inhabitants; nevertheless some produce is exported from Gran Tarajal on the south-west coast.

During the last fifteen years, Fuerteventura has developed a small tourist industry, but mass tourism is unlikely to invade in the near future because of the acute shortage of fresh water. The island appeals to visitors who love sun, sand and tranquillity; the windsurfing is excellent and the 'blue ribbon' event at Sotovento in July each year attracts the world's best.

As on Lanzarote, the old capital of the island is well inland: it was founded by Jean de Bethencourt, who named it Betancuria after himself. It boasts a fine church, some attractive sixteenth- and seventeenth-century colonial architecture and a fair amount of greenery including mature palm trees. Other interesting old towns in the north of the island are La Oliva, with a distinguished mansion known as Casa de los Coroneles (House of the Colonels), Pájara and Antigua. The present capital, Puerto del Rosario, lies on the east coast: until 1957 it was known as Puerto de las Cabras (Goats), but it was felt that this name did little for the town's image! The town has smartened itself up in recent years and has adequate shopping facilities as well as a number of hotels, the most notable being the Parador Nacional de Fuerteventura overlooking the sandy beach of Playa Blanca north of the airport.

Fuerteventura has twice known immigration: in the 1730s refugees from the volcanic eruptions on Lanzarote fled there, and, two hundred years later, opponents of General Franco were exiled on the island. The most eminent of these was Miguel de Unamuno, the Basque poet, whose presence on the island is commemorated by a huge white monument on a mountainside just south of Tindaya.

A day's visit from Lanzarote will almost certainly make you want to return, and perhaps to visit the offshore Isla de Lobos also. Virtually uninhabited, this island is part of a nature reserve and offers lovely walks, fine sandy coves and some of the best snorkelling in the Canaries. The name means 'Seal Island': Lanzarote's conqueror, Gadifer de la Salle, was marooned here by his mutinous troops for several weeks without food and water after a seal-hunting trip. You are less likely to see seals on the island today, but keep your eyes open just in case.

LA GRACIOSA

The small island of La Graciosa lies off the north-west tip of Lanzarote, separated from it by the deep channel of El Río, only a kilometre wide at its narrowest point. To make an excursion to the island you must drive to the small port of Órzola on the north coast, from which a modern launch (run by Lineas Maritimas Romero, tel: 842055, fax: 842069) leaves at 10.00, 12.00, 17.00 and 18.30, returning at 08.00, 11.00, 16.00 and 18.00. The trip to La Graciosa takes 25 minutes: it may be cancelled if the sea is too rough, but in fact this only happens three or four times a year. The cost of the crossing is 1700 ptas return (children 850) and the ferry puts into the sheltered harbour of Caleta del Sebo where there is a handful of bars, three *pensiones*, a 'supermarket' and a bank. Mountain bikes can be hired from a couple of outlets by the water's edge.

La Graciosa is nine km. long and four wide at its broader end; the total area is 25 sq. km. Less than one thousand people live on the island, mostly in Caleta del Sebo, and many of the working population cross daily to Lanzarote. For those whose livelihood still depends on fishing, life has hardly changed over the centuries; there is no noise or air pollution nor any tarmacked roads. Agriculture is almost impossible as the island is so sandy and windswept. Tourism is unlikely to gain a foothold here, and La Graciosa attracts divers, underwater photographers, anglers and those in search of total tranquillity.

The coast is rocky but punctuated by white sandy beaches, the most magnificent (and most visited) being Playa de las Conchas in the north-west; Montaña Clara looms offshore, and beyond it the inhospitable islet of Alegranza, most northerly of all the Canaries, is home only to a colony of puffins. The hinterland of La Graciosa is barren and rises to four distinct peaks, the summits of old volcanoes: the highest of these is Pedro Barba at 266m.

Caleta del Sebo ('Greasy Cove') owes its name to the discovery of whale blubber on the beach, and Pedro Barba is named after a fifteenth-century Spanish crusader who landed here and declared himself King of the Canary Islands. He had been sent by Juan II of Castile to prevent Maciot de Bethencourt from selling the islands to Portugal (see p. 52). There is a reference to this incident in Cervantes' *Don Quijote*.

As La Graciosa lay close to the main sea route between Europe and South America it became a familiar landfall for pirates and privateers eager to intercept shipping laden with gold from the New World. Inevitably, rumours of treasure buried there abound, and there is even a theory that Robert Louis Stevenson may have been inspired to write *Treasure Island* when he heard the story of a British ship, laden with wealth, being chased to La Graciosa by pirates. Before they were set upon by their pursuers, the crew managed to bury their treasure and never revealed its location despite being tortured to death. The ship's cabin boy, however, miraculously escaped and returned to England. He kept his knowledge a secret until shortly before he died, but he was then too old to give clear directions as to the treasure's whereabouts.

Desert islands will always attract romantics, and the possibility of undiscovered loot makes La Graciosa a fascinating place to dream on!

Children's Lanzarote

Besides the obvious attractions of its beaches, Lanzarote has plenty to offer families with young children. All the resorts have children's playgrounds of some sort (and amusement arcades for older children). In Puerto del Carmen, next to the Hotel San Antonio, is an 18-hole **mini-golf** course, open 10.00–18.00 (price 500 ptas a round); two blocks west of here, but also on the sea-front road, is the **Aquarium** and **Reptilarium**. This features a continuous video of marine life in a nearby sea grotto, as well as tanks of colourful fish; the reptilarium is home to tortoises, snakes and small crocodiles (tel: 513076). The **Acualanza water park** in Costa Teguise attracts excursions from all parts of Lanzarote; it has heated swimming pools and half a dozen water chutes and flumes of various designs. Sunbathing and shaded areas are available, as are first aid facilities; the park is open 10.00–18.00 daily (1450 ptas, 700 for children aged 2–12, sunbeds 200 ptas, changing rooms 50 ptas, tel: 592128). Another excursion with child appeal is the **Guinate Tropical Park** (open 10.00–17.00 daily, see pp. 114), a small zoo containing wallabies, meerkats, chipmunk and coatis and an aviary of 300 birds: performing macaws and cockatoos give shows throughout the day.

Shopping

Shops on Lanzarote are mostly open from 09.00–13.00 and 16.00–19.30 (09.00–13.00 only on Sats): many shops, however, especially supermarkets, open for much longer hours. There are small supermarkets in almost every village and in the tourist resorts, of course, they abound. Since most visitors to Lanzarote are likely to be staying in self-catering apartments, these shops tend to stock a wide variety of goods, including hardware, stationery, etc. The duty-free status of the Canaries means that even the smallest supermarket will stock an ambitious variety of alcoholic drinks and tobacco products. The lowest prices are to be

Souvenir shopping

found in Arrecife and at Centro Discount Maxi, the hypermarket just south-west of Teguise on the Mozaga road (open Mon–Sat 09.00–20.00). The English Food Market near Güime sells only British foodstuffs, including a range of vegan and vegetarian products (open Mon–Sat 09.30–13.30, tel: 815914).

For souvenir shopping, hand-embroidered tablecloths, napkins, handkerchieves, etc., are predominant. Fine embroidery is a craft practised throughout the archipelago, and each island has its own traditional designs; all types are available in Lanzarote's tourist shops and shopkeepers are pleased to advise as to which designs are the local ones. Do feel free to ask: some of the cheaper embroidered items in fact originate in the Far East, so to be sure your purchase is Canarian it is as well to check. Authentic Lanzarotean handiwork is sold from the Taller de Artesanía, Haría (see p. 113), from Per Eckhoff's interesting shop opposite the *taller* – Herr Eckhoff sells a very palatable wine made from his own grapes, propagates and sells cacti, as well as home-made marmalade and local artwork – and from Artesanía Lanzaroteña, next to the Acatife restaurant in Teguise.

Popular souvenirs include items of woven palm, especially large hats of the kind worn by the workers in the fields; the *timple*, a five-stringed guitar unique to the Canaries and mostly made in Teguise; local pottery; rag dolls in local costume; leather goods (usually imported from the mainland or Africa) and, most typically Lanzarotean, small items of olivine (peridot), the greenish semi-precious stone found in the lava fields (see also p. 107).

The César Manrique Foundation has developed a mini-industry of souvenirs made to the artist's designs: framed prints, posters, tiles, T-shirts and jewellery are on sale at the Foundation's shops: these can be found at José Betancort 26, Arrecife (open 10.00–13.00); Otilia Diaz 10, Arrecife (open 10.00–13.00, 15.00–18.00), La Lonja, Plaza 18 de Julio, Teguise (open 11.00–13.00, 15.00–18.00, Sats and Suns 11.00–13.00) and at Avenida de las Playas 47, Puerto del Carmen (open 10.00–13.00, 18.00–21.30).

The Canaries' traditional duty-free status is not as advantageous as it once was for visitors; basically all it means nowadays is that the IVA (VAT) charged in mainland Spain on luxury goods is waived in the archipelago. The effect is that cameras, radios, tape recorders, calculators, watches, electronic items, some perfumes and jewellery, tobacco and alcoholic drinks are up to 25 per cent cheaper than in peninsular Spain (though you will probably still have to pay UK VAT when bringing some of these items home).

Customs allowances on returning to the UK are not currently the same as they are from elsewhere in the EU: you are allowed 2 litres of still table wine, *plus* 1 litre of spirits over 22 per cent vol *or* 2 litres of liqueurs/fortified wines under 22 per cent vol *or* a further 2 litres of wine; perfume, 60 cc/ml; toilet water, 250 cc/ml; tobacco, 200 cigarettes *or* 100 cigarillos *or* 50 cigars *or* 250 grammes of tobacco. Only £36's worth of other goods may be imported. These allowances are the same whether you buy on the island (usually cheaper) or on the aircraft flying home.

TOURING ROUTES

Lanzarote is an island well suited to touring by car. Not only is car rental cheap – a week's hire costs little more than a couple of organized excursions plus the odd taxi between towns – but Lanzarote's size and configuration mean that the energetic tourist can, if he or she wishes, drive along almost every road on the island during a week's stay, and thus get a rich impression of the variety of scenery and landscapes it has to offer.

The routes that follow should be regarded as very flexible. They start and end at Puerto del Carmen, since this resort is still by far the most populous on Lanzarote, but directions from Playa Blanca and the Costa Teguise are given at the end. Incorporated in each route are a variety of subsidiary excursions (with the time it takes to make them at a leisurely pace included): so you can choose how many of these, if any, you wish to add to the main itinerary. With a reasonable map of Lanzarote (several are available in the UK or in the island's shops) you can easily work out combinations and permutations of the routes: our purpose is merely to ensure that, if the weather is good and the beaches inviting but you nevertheless want to see more of this fascinating island than just the tourist resorts, you can cover the main attractions of the island as directly as possible.

Everyone who visits Lanzarote will want to tour the Timanfaya National Park, so we begin with a brief separate account of this experience. The tour of the park, which takes about an hour, can however be combined with either the Central or the Southern route if time is short.

TIMANFAYA NATIONAL PARK

'On the first day of September, between 9 and 10 in the evening, the earth opened up near Timanfaya two leagues from Yaiza and an enormous mountain arose from the bosom of the earth. Flames flew upwards from the top which continued to burn for nineteen days.'

With these words Don Andrés Lorenzo Curbelo, the parish

priest of Yaiza, described the beginning of the massive volcanic eruptions that began in 1730 and created the mountain range now known as the Montañas del Fuego de Timanfaya. The eruptions lasted for six years, and in the process an ever-widening circle of devastation was created in what had until then been one of the most fertile regions on the island. Ten villages, including Timanfaya – some 420 houses – were entirely swallowed up, and, when the lava finally cooled, an area of about 200 square kilometres had been covered. The once fertile cereal fields had been transformed into a sea of ash and clinker, and 32 new craters thrust up from the desolated land. Much of this is now the National Park of Timanfaya, and visiting it is the single most celebrated and unmissable excursion on Lanzarote.

If you are visiting the National Park as a separate excursion the simplest approach from Puerto del Carmen is via Yaiza, where a signposted right turn off the bypass brings you very soon to the first of the wrought-iron 'devil' signs that are the symbol of the park. Shortly afterwards you will come to a large car park on your left. Here there is a small picnic area and a bar, but the reason for the car park's existence is that this is where the celebrated dromedary rides begin and end. You will probably see lines of the impassive beasts kneeling on the gritty lava with green wooden seats slung either side of their humps. The trip up the side of the mountains into a crater and back costs 1300 ptas and lasts some 25 minutes (no reduction for children). There have been very few mishaps on this journey and there really is no reason for any but the most nervous to be deterred from taking a dromedary ride. Passengers sit in the seats on either side of the hump; the only safety strap is a piece of string, so a sense of balance is useful, especially when the camel gets up off its knees with a sudden forwards jerk. After this moment of unease, however, most people find the ride an exhilarating and often uproarious experience. The rides operate from 09.00–16.00 daily.

After the dromedary station, the road continues north through fields of grotesquely twisted lava (the so-called *pahoehoe* type, from the Hawaiian word meaning 'ropey'). The entrance to the park is reached a few km further on, signalled by a further wrought-iron devil. There is a barrier here and there can be considerable queueing in the road outside the entrance for private vehicles: so it is a good idea to arrive early in the day if you can. The entrance fee of 900 ptas per person includes a place on one of the special buses which tour the 'Ruta de los Volcanes'. You then drive through an unearthly landscape of surprisingly varied colours from plain black through browns and reds to the whitish green of the lichen (*liquén*) which is the only plant life that can grow on the lava. After 2 km the road loops round to the left and you arrive at the Islote de Hilario; an *islote* on Lanzarote is an outcrop of land rising above the lava, and this one is said to derive its name from a hermit named Hilario who returned to this devastated area after the eruptions and lived here for fifty years with only a donkey for company. Now an attractive circular building constructed of lava blocks and glass (and designed, of course, by César Manrique, the artist/architect responsible for so many of Lanzarote's attractions) stands here, containing a restaurant and snack bar, with toilets and a small shop. The restaurant specialises in meat grilled directly over the heat from the volcano; the fig tree in the centre is claimed as a descendant of one planted by Hilario.

There is plentiful parking here despite the crowds of visitors. Leave the car and inspect the displays that are staged on the Islote de Hilario to demonstrate the heat that still rages just below the surface. The temperature inside the mountain is 600° C and even a few inches below the surface it is 100° C: tests have shown that the ground temperature at Islote de Hilario has not decreased substantially for 200 years. First, visitors will see an attendant thrust a bundle of dried furze into a pit in the ground, whereupon it bursts into

The *malpaís* at Timanfaya

flames a few seconds later. You may also be invited to take a handful of red gravel he picks up from the ground: most people drop this with a shriek, as it is unbearably hot. The displays culminate in the guide's pouring a small bucket of water into one or two of several pipes sunk into the ground. Seconds later, a satisfactorily high geyser of steam shoots into the air. Photographers should be warned that the geyser erupts extremely suddenly and can go as high as 40 feet, so quick reactions are needed to capture it on film!

The Islote is the starting point for the Ruta de los Volcanes (Volcanic Route), which begins as a narrow twisting roadway carved deep into the jagged lava from which breathtaking close-ups of the desolation can be seen. Perhaps sensibly, it is not permitted to follow this route in a private car; instead it is necessary to take one of the skilfully driven buses, on which a recorded commentary is played in Spanish, English and German: they depart every few minutes at busy times, and pause occasionally for photographs, but the number of visitors nowadays means it is no longer possible for them to stop long enough for passengers to get out and drink in the scene.

The trip round the volcanic route is a nine-kilometre itinerary which takes about 40 minutes: it is unquestionably unique and even those whose interest in geology is minimal are impressed and awestruck by the views it offers. You will see such features as volcanic chimneys, fumaroles, *hornitos* ('ovens') and the serene 'Valley of Tranquillity', whose smooth sides look like enormous tawny sand dunes but are in fact composed of millions of volcanic *lapilli*: quite lifeless, the valley's silence makes the tourist bus seem a noisy intruder. A pause is also made beside the 'Raven's Crater', regarded by geologists as a classic example of its type. This grim and desolate landscape strikes many visitors as hellish and depressing at first, despite the occasional evidence of returning plant life. But many more become gradually sensible of its weird and tragic beauty, as the play of the light and the varying colours of the lava are appreciated. The extraordinary landscapes of Fire Mountain are certainly an impressive spectacle – it is said that early American astronauts were shown photographs of the region to familiarize them with the sort of scenery they might expect to find on the moon, and 'lunar' is inevitably the adjective that comes to most people's minds when contemplating the volcanic wastes of Timanfaya.

Because of the need to time your arrival at the Islote de Hilario satisfactorily in relation to the departure of the next coach, you may feel that Timanfaya is one excursion where an organized coach trip has advantages over going independently, since with an organized trip your own coach will take you round the Volcanic Route as soon as you have seen the displays. However, the Islote complex offers enough diversions to help the independent traveller pass the time if he has just missed a bus.

Strolling at will in the National Park is not permitted; in such an inhospitable landscape this is a sensible prohibition, and most people would agree after stumbling a few yards on the harsh and unstable lava that a walk is a pleasure easily foregone. Guided nature trails through the park can be arranged for small groups, however; for information tel: 840057, 811060 or 801500.

The Timanfaya National Park is open from 09.00 until 17.45 every day. (The last bus round the Ruta de los Volcanes departs at 17.00.) It is possible to visit the area in the evenings, but only on an organized excursion (16.20 to 22.00) to view the sunset. This trip usually includes a meal with folk music in the Islote de Hilario restaurant.

After leaving the park, it is well worth paying a visit to the **Visitors' Centre** (Centro de Visitantes e Interpretación de Mancha Blanca), a few km further north. Opened in February 1996, this new exhibition centre is a model of its kind, with genuinely engrossing displays explaining the geology, natural history and traditional life of Lanzarote. Admission is free but you will need to purchase disposable earphones (200 ptas from the excellent souvenir shop) to hear the commentary to the audio-visual show in any language other than Spanish. As well as the informative displays the Centre even offers the experience of a simulated eruption (open 09.00–17.00 daily).

[From Playa Blanca the Park is best reached via Yaiza, as described above. From Costa Teguise it is simpler to head north for Tahiche, where you cross the Teguise–Arrecife road and make for San Bartolomé. Here turn right for Tiagua, then left for Mancha Blanca and the entrance to the Park.]

Arrecife

Lanzarote's capital is home to some 40,000 people, almost half the population. The name of the city means 'reef' and a glance at the map shows that it is protected from the open sea by a series of offshore islets. Arrecife is a relatively young city, which became the capital only in 1852: previously Teguise, despite the constant depredations of pirates, enjoyed that distinction. But as overseas trade gradually developed, the inland towns (which had provided a relatively safe refuge from seaborne raiders in earlier eras) began to decline in favour of the coastal settlements, of which Arrecife with its excellent natural harbours was foremost.

The town has grown steadily since the arrival of mass tourism. Its main landmark remains the multi-storey Gran Hotel on the seafront (partially destroyed by fire on 19 November 1994 and at the time of writing still the subject of considerable debate as to its future). This is the only high-rise building in the town – César Manrique is said to have been so appalled by its construction (he was away in New York at the time) that, anticipating the possibility of a Manhattan-type skyline in Arrecife, he implored the Cabildo (the island's governing body) to allow him to oversee future building.

As a result there has been no further high-rise building in Arrecife, which, though scarcely an elegant city, is an unpretentious, bustling, friendly place, untidy and traffic-choked in places but for the most part homogeneous. The streets are narrow, many of them are not named and the majority are one-way, making negotiating the city in a car somewhat difficult.

The waterfront features a short but attractive *paseo* in a small park with seats and trees (a kiosk here houses the tourist information office, see p.26). The seafront promenade runs from the Red Cross building (formerly the island's *parador* and worth a glimpse for the lively Manrique murals on the ground floor) to the **Las Bolas** bridge, a drawbridge so named from the cannon balls on top of the entry pillars. The bridge leads to a causeway linking one of Arrecife's offshore islets, the Islote de los Ingleses, to the city. On this small island stands the **Castillo de San Gabriel**, rebuilt by the Italian architect Torriani in 1599 on the orders of Philip II as a defence against Berber pirate raids. The Castillo houses Lanzarote's Archaeological Museum (open 09.00–14.45 Mon–Fri, admission 100 ptas), displaying small archaeological finds and incised stones from the Zonzamas site (see p.132), and primitive pottery from the *malpaís* (badlands) de Corona. In the fort's outer galleries the massive walls display plans and sketches of various archaeological sites on the island. There is a good view of the town from the roof and the opportunity to ring the fort's bell. (There is also a car park by the Castillo, which you may find useful if you are visiting the town in a car. Other parking opportunities are limited: metered spaces can be found along the waterfront and there is some free parking on the eastern sign of the Charco de San Ginés.)

The main shopping street, **León y Castillo,** runs inland from the seafront, beginning almost opposite the Las Bolas bridge with the tiled headquarters of the Cabildo (island government). Most of the banks are located here, and a variety of useful shops: prices here are usually lower than in the tourist resorts. Further on, towards the harbour, the Calle Liebre is the site of a small market, with a fish market in a smaller building.

Two blocks inland stands Arrecife's main church, the **Iglesia de San Ginés**, in the small shady Plaza de las Palmas. A large eighteenth-century structure, it was originally a hermitage, becoming the parish church in 1798; the interior features a fine ceiling of dark wood and black basalt pillars contrasting with the plain white walls. It is the centre of important festivities at Corpus Christi and, around 22 August each year. In Calle Insp. Luis Martín, between the church and León y Castillo, can be found the best bookshop (Spanish titles only) in the town, the Librería el Puente.

Behind the church is a wide natural yacht basin, the **Charco de San Ginés,** a tranquil part of the city with a few waterside bars where you may often see egrets. The four-screen Atlántida Cinema is here and the Charco is the scene of a market on Saturdays.

The main harbours of Arrecife lie to the north: the shallow fishing harbour of **Naos,** home to the largest fishing fleet in the Canaries and the seventh largest in all Spain, and further on **Puerto de los Mármoles** (Marbles), where larger ships put in. As the closest port in the Canaries to Africa and Spain, its volume of traffic is exceeded only by that of Las Palmas. There are immense shoals of fish very close at hand and fishing, with the associated industries of canning and salting, has traditionally been an important source of Arrecife's wealth, though only one canning factory remains open today.

A stroll around the streets of central Arrecife reveals plenty of interest. At José Betancourt 26–33 is '**El Almacén**' where César Manrique converted an old warehouse into an art gallery: on the other side of the road, his old design offices (open 10.00–13.00 Mon–Fri) display prints of his work and a few originals (a further Manrique shop can be found nearby in calle Otilia Diaz, see p.84). Back on the waterfront, the slightly scruffy **Casa de Cultura** (named for the eminent Lanzaroteño historian, Agustín de la Hoz) opposite the Tourist Office holds periodic exhibitions and a little further east is the Blas Cabrera Museum, opened in 1995 in the eighteenth-century **Casa de los Arroyo,** one of the oldest houses in the town. Cabrera, who was born in Arrecife in 1878, did pioneering work on the magnetic properties of materials and the structure of the atom: his seminal books included *Principio de Relatividad* and *El Átomo*. The museum displays panels explaining his contribution to science and describing his life and contacts with the likes of Albert Einstein (open 10.30–13.30, 18.30–20.30 Mon–Fri, admission free). Also on the waterfront, to the west and opposite the Casino, is the Pastelería Lolita, an excellent spot for a pastry, a coffee or an ice cream.

South of the city lie two good beaches, **Playa del Reducto** (behind which buses depart for the southern part of the island) and **Playa del Cable**: both are popular with the townsfolk, and recent determined efforts to clear up a pollution problem have resulted in Playa del Reducto earning a Blue Flag. It is planned that in due course a coastal promenade will run all the way between these beaches and Puerto del Carmen.

Route 1 Central

PUERTO DEL CARMEN – MÁCHER – UGA – LA GERIA – MOZAGA – TEGUISE – TAHICHE – PUERTO DEL CARMEN

[60 km/38 miles – about three hours without detours]

From Puerto del Carmen take the road north-west up the hill from the crossroads in the old town (Banco Central on the corner), following signs for Mácher.

When the developments of Puerto del Carmen finally cease, you will find yourself driving through an area of intensive cultivation surrounding **Mácher**: beans, peas, sweetcorn, cabbages, potatoes and the ubiquitous onions grow in small fields covered over with the porous black lava granules, *picón*. The rows of plants are often sheltered from the wind by low barriers of stones, twigs or even orange boxes laid on their sides. The village of Mácher sprawls along the main Arrecife–Yaiza road (GC 720) which you reach about five minutes out of Puerto del Carmen. The usual low, dazzlingly white Lanzarotean houses are scattered along the road on a gentle slope with views down to Puerto del Carmen and the coast.

Turn left onto the GC 720 (signposted 'Yaiza'), a good fast road through undulating hills that are tinged with green early in the year. There are distant views of the islands of Lobos and Fuerteventura to the south, and after 2 km a turning to the left leads past the large Yaiza Senior School to reach Lanzarote's spanking new **Puerto Calero** yacht marina. Planned eventually to incorporate a 4-star hotel and *urbanización*, it offers berths for around 150 boats, with attendant facilities including workshops and a dry dock.

Detour: 5 km after Mácher a minor road signposted 'Playa Quemada' takes you down to the small fishing village of that name. Still largely unaffected by tourism, **Playa Quemada** is a sleepy, slightly scruffy little hamlet: it has a small, secluded dark beach, Playa de la Arena, and the road down to it affords pleasant views of Fuerteventura and the Ajaches mountain range to the south. Also on the road down you can sometimes see a herd of young dromedaries grazing unsupervised on the sparse and

Agriculture at Uga

thorny vegetation on the hillside, with every appearance of relish. [6 km/4 m: 20 minutes]

About 7 km from Mácher you reach the quiet, unpretentious village of **Uga**, bypassed by the main road. The original village was completely engulfed by the volcanic eruptions of the eighteenth century, and the modern settlement was rebuilt literally on the ashes of the old, which lie some 30 feet below. Home base of the camels which carry tourists up the mountains of Timanfaya, Uga has an attractively simple modern church, San Isidro Labrador, standing in front of a new plaza that is a riot of geraniums planted among blindingly white stone benches.

Uga boasts several restaurants, including the Restaurant Timanfaya which has a large room used for displays of Canarian folk dancing and wrestling (see p. 76). These 'Fiestas Canarias' usually occur twice a week and tickets can be obtained through almost any agent or tour operator. They probably offer the best opportunity to see the local wrestling, which is the traditional sport of Lanzarote. Tourist visitors are regularly invited to join in the fun. The rules, however, are complicated and the locals extremely competent, so this is not usually advisable! Another of Uga's claims to fame is the smoking of fish, especially salmon, which regularly appears on better-class menus on the island. You can buy some here, if you wish, at the smoking house on the left of the road to Yaiza just past the town – the salmon is about 4600 ptas a kilo.

Leave the GC 720 at Uga (signposted 'La Geria/ Teguise'). The second or third turning to the left immediately after this will take you into the centre of Uga, should you wish to look around a little. To continue the route, find the Teguise road again (the LZ 30 or GC 730, now signposted 'Teguise por La Geria'), an older, narrower road without markings which climbs briefly around the back of Uga to reach the intriguing **La Geria** region a few minutes later. This is the celebrated agricultural area, covered in semi-circular walls of lava, which most tellingly attests to the resilience, resourcefulness and sheer industry of the Lanzarotean peasant farmer.

For acre after acre, the hillsides are covered with these half-moons, some almost silted over by the action of the wind, some obviously recently constructed. Each wall shelters a plant from the prevailing north-easterly winds, usually a vine (which may look dead early in the year but rapidly puts out leaves as the spring advances), but sometimes a fig or even an almond tree, growing in a deep pit which has been partially filled in with a layer of *picón*, the porous granules of black ash which make Lanzarotean agriculture so distinctive.

These granules, so dry in appearance, act like sponges, absorbing any moisture that is available in the air (even on the many rainless days there is usually some degree of dew overnight) and feeding it gradually to the plant beneath. Interestingly, this use of *picón* is not particularly ancient; for many years before its introduction, sand was used for the same purpose, and farmers would pray for easterly winds to bring a layer of sand from the Sahara, 112 km. away, to protect their fields from sun and drought. *Picón* is far more effective, however, being the nearest thing to a sponge that the mineral world can produce. The idea of using it methodically may have been suggested by the observation that plants did well after being covered by a light layer of ash in a volcanic eruption. In any event the discovery of the value of *picón* must rank as a major advance in the history of Lanzarote.*

* *This porosity of the lava is quite hard to comprehend: it is said that in a building constructed of lava blocks a wilting houseplant placed near a wall will revive within a few hours as a result of absorbing the moisture retained in the wall.*

The La Geria area is an important source of the unusual and potent *malvasía* wine of Lanzarote. A feature of the landscape is that instead of being dotted with small villages, there are only a few, quite large establishments, many of which offer the opportunity to taste their wines. The grape harvest is in early September.

Detour About 8 km from Uga a recently metalled road signposted 'Tinajo por Tinguatón' heads off straight across the lava fields on the left. This little-used road is worth taking if you have the time, as it affords spectacular views of the low volcanic hills all around, the most individual of these being the red-sided Montaña Ortiz to your right. Also visible are the wonderfully multi-coloured Pico Partido to your left, the edge of a collapsed crater, and further on the sooty sides of the Los Rostros range. Despite the recent upgrade, this is still a lonely stretch of road, which offers a real opportunity to experience the majesty of the *malpaís*. If you fancy a walk up to the rim of a crater this is a good place to try it: there are several within easy reach of the road and no 'No Pasar' notices. And if you spot any rabbits eating the pale lichen that grows on the lava hereabouts you will merely be confirming one of Lanzarote's favourite myths!

After 6 km the road surmounts a small rise: suddenly cultivated fields appear and the west coast comes into view ahead – in the early months of the year, the contrast with the barrenness behind you is dramatic. At **Mancha Blanca**, reached next, the lava flow from Tinguatón is said to have been halted or diverted by the miraculous intervention of Our Lady of the Sorrows, thus saving the village from extinction. The Ermita de los Dolores to the right of the road as you leave the town commemorates the villagers' gratitude. An imposing structure with a cupola and a cool, plain white interior, it is the centre in mid-September each year of a massive crafts fair and one of Lanzarote's most important fiestas, attended by half the island. Normally Mancha Blanca is a quiet though sizeable village, surrounded by fields planted with per-fectly spaced rows of vegetables, protected by drystone walls.

Turning left here would bring you to the entrance to the Timanfaya National Park, but our route entails a right turn in the town (signposted 'Tiagua/La Vegueta'). This takes you along an unremarkable stretch of road through an agricultural area (growing mostly watermelons, sweet potatoes and maize) around the small unmarked village of La Vegueta. After driving through this fertile country for about 6 km, a crossroads is reached at Tiagua. Straight on, the road leads to Muñique and Sóo, past the eighteenth-century Ermita de la Virgen de Perpetuo Socorro, and a turning to the right shortly after the crossroads brings you to the excellent **Museo Agrícola El Patio** (Country Farm Museum) opened in 1995 (see pp.65–6), distinguishable by its prominent windmills. To resume the route, however, turn right at these crossroads (signposted 'Arrecife') and continue southwards through Tao, a pleasant agricultural town on a windswept ridge affording views of Teguise and the Famara cliffs to the north with the uninhabited island of Alegranza in the distance, until the main route is rejoined by turning left at the roundabout in Mozaga. [18 km/11 m: about 25 minutes]

The cultivated lava fields now give way to volcanic *malpais* with the coloured mountains of the Timanfaya Park as a backdrop on your left and, nearer the road, two smaller volcanic peaks, known as Montaña Negra and Juan Bello (Handsome John!). Immediately after the village of Masdache, the headquarters of the **El Grifo** wine concern, founded in 1775, offers further opportunities to sample and buy wine (at prices about 25 per cent cheaper than in supermarkets), plus a skilfully laid-out wine museum displaying nineteenth- and early twentieth-century wine-making equipment (open 10.00–18.00 Mon–Fri).

Approximately 15 km from Uga, Mozaga, the next village, lies at the centre of the island and is the site of the **Monumento el Campesino**, César Manrique's soaring white sculpture of water cans and fragments of boats, which was erected in 1968 to celebrate fertility and the heroic tenacity of the Lanzarotean peasant in wresting a living from his unpromising land. Near it a small cluster of buildings in the typical Lanzarote style house a museum, pottery, wine shop and a restaurant where a buffet of local foods is served – well worth a stop. Mozaga is still wine-growing country and the local *malvasía* rivals El Grifo in popularity. After admiring the view of the monument, go straight over the roundabout and continue on the same road

(GC 730) towards Teguise, distinguishable ahead by its church tower and the castle perched on the hill above it. The road now traverses the central plain linking the northern and southern mountain ranges. Flat sandy soils extend on both sides of the road with views of the Famara cliffs to the north, rising to the Peñas del Chache, Lanzarote's highest point.

Detour Take a road going off to your left 4 km after Mozaga (signposted 'La Caleta de Famara') for a look at the magnificent beach at the end. It leads through the sandy plain known as El Jable, arriving after about 9 km at the majestic sweep of Playa de Famara, a long golden beach backed partly by a large area of sand dunes and partly by the towering cliffs known as the **Riscos de Famara** which rise almost sheer to the highest point on the island, the Peñas del Chache (670 m). This is a wild and romantic area, only slightly marred by an unobtrusive development of low semicircular bungalows. It is almost always windy, and the long breakers are extremely popular with windsurfers, though only the most expert can make headway here. Swimming is dangerous more often than not. In the bay the upper parts of a wrecked ship are clearly visible: driven onshore in 1981 with a cargo of cement, the vessel remains to bear witness to the strength of the winds here. Nobody has troubled to salvage it yet and it seems unlikely now that anyone ever will. One can drive some way along under the cliffs (skirting the back of the bungalow development) for further views, and a little-used footpath runs along the cliff face about halfway up before petering out in a ravine. The road which used to run right to the northern tip of the island from Famara beach, however, is no longer in use.

At the southern end of the beach the small fishing village of **La Caleta** (where César Manrique spent his childhood) is pleasantly scruffy and offers several restaurants should a lunch break be indicated at this point. To resume the route, either retrace your steps back to the GC 730 or, if you are feeling adventurous, take the old road into Teguise which branches off to the left 2 km out of Playa de Famara. No longer surfaced or maintained, the road is poor but can be used with care; it winds along the southern slopes of the hills and offers excellent views of

The plaza at Teguise

the centre of the island, reaching Teguise after 6 km via the Ermita de San Rafael. Otherwise, drive back to the GC 730 and turn left to reach the city after a further 3 km. [20 km/12 m: 30 minutes]

Teguise, named after the daughter of Guadarfía, last king of Lanzarote (who married Maciot de Bethencourt, see p.52), was for centuries the island's capital and is still known to older Lanzaroteños simply as 'La Villa'. It is a dignified town of stone-paved streets, churches and colonial-style houses often featuring fine doors, window frames and balconies of carved wood: the whole city has been designated a National Monument. A plan is available from the Archivo Histórico, and a stroll through the streets is rewarding. Tranquil today, these streets have seen violence and brutality in their time: for many centuries Teguise was the nearest civilized settlement to the North African coast and in consequence was constantly subject to raiding by pirates and slave-catchers, as street names such as that of the Callejón de la Sangre (where many women and children were massacred in 1586) testify.

The town centres on an irregularly shaped *plaza*, the scene of a lively market on Sundays (see p.68), dominated by the tower of the massively built church of San Miguel (strictly N.S. de Guadalupe), one of the oldest in the Canaries. Begun in 1428 and sacked several times in the sixteenth and seventeenth centuries, the church has a large and airy interior, though the neo-gothic details in brilliant white plaster resembling royal icing combined with Corinthian pillars, romanesque arches and a painted ceiling, produce a somewhat disharmonious effect. Opposite stands the sixteenth-century Palacio Spínola, constructed of lava blocks and timber. It is open to the public (300 ptas) and houses periodic art exhibitions. Other monumental buildings in the town include the churches of San Francisco (also sixteenth-century, with an ornamental spiral staircase, ceiling and altar screen of polished wood) and Vera Cruz (containing a sixteenth-century crucifix). The imposing Convent of Santo Domingo, founded in 1726 and recently

House at Teguise

restored (during the work over 100 skeletons were discovered in a crypt), is now used for occasional art exhibitions.
Private buildings of interest include the eighteenth-century
Casa Torres and the Casa Parroquial, a seventeenth-century
barracks, the Herrera-Rojas Palace, the old residence of the
Marquises of Lanzarote (which housed the island's archives
until their destruction by North African raiders) and La
Cilla, the old tithe-barn opposite San Miguel, which is now
a bank. An area of waste ground behind San Miguel used to
contain the Gran Mareta, a large reservoir from which water
was distributed all over the island.

Teguise has some excellent restaurants and shops, including a César Manrique shop and the Artesanía Lanzaroteña
in the *plaza*. It is also a centre for the manufacture of the
timple, a small five-stringed guitar also known as '*el
camellito*', that is much used in Canarian folk music. Several
craftsmen make them in the town, among them Antonio
Lemes Hernández, who can sometimes be seen at work in a
garage in Calle Flores near the Spínola Palace. The writer,
critic and playwright 'Ángel Guerra' (José Betancort
Cabrera, 1774–1806) was a native of Teguise; so was José
Clavijo y Fajardo (1726–1806), founder of the influential
periodical *El Pensador*, whose life inspired works by Goethe
and Beaumarchais.

Looming over the town to the east is the very ancient
volcanic crater of Guanapay, surmounted by the sixteenth-
century **Castillo de Santa Bárbara**. Built by the Italian
architect Leonardo Torriani in 1596 on the site of an earlier
tower, this fort fulfilled the vital function of keeping a look-
out for pirates and other unwelcome visitors. The fort
houses the Museo del Emigrante (see p. 65), and a metalled
road leads up the hill towards it. The ascent makes a pleasant
walk, however, if the day is not too hot (about 25 minutes to
the fort), rewarding the climber with magnificent views in
all directions from the summit. In winter and early spring,
if there has been any rain at all, the road is bordered with
wild flowers: milkwort, 'boots and shoes', spurges of various
kinds, restharrow, sedums and the ubiquitous purple of
viper's bugloss, as well as many other small rock plants.
Butterflies abound, too, at this time of the year. At the top,
the ancient crater forms a green bowl and an effective
suntrap on windy days. You can walk right around the rim
of the crater, enjoying views of the Fire Mountain region
and the west coast, with the hills above Haría and La

Graciosa and the other islets to the north; the other side brings the east coast into view from Costa Teguise past Arrecife down to the Ajaches mountains in the south – on a clear day even Fuerteventura can be seen. The whole walk, including the circuit of the crater, takes about an hour.

From Teguise take the main Arrecife road south, past Nazaret (originally a small village, now much expanded by the 'Oasis de Nazaret' development which catches the sun on the slopes of the hill to your left). After 6 km you reach **Tahiche**, an elegant town containing several large and attractively designed villas, most famously, César Manrique's own **Taro de Tahiche**, parts of which are actually within the lava: now open to the public (see p.64), it has become one of Lanzarote's most visited attractions.

Turn right at the roundabout just beyond the Taro, dominated by an enormous wind-driven Manrique sculpture, and head south. Arrecife now comes into view, and 3.5 km from Tahiche you reach the ring road around the capital, where you may choose to go straight on in order to take a look at the city. If not, bear right (signed 'Aeropuerto') and follow the bypass to rejoin the GC 720 which skirts the resort of Playa Honda; shortly after passing the airport, follow signs for Puerto del Carmen which you will reach, via its burgeoning satellites of Matagorda (once an important area of salt-pans) and Los Pocillos, about 7 km further on (be sure to veer right off this road when Puerto del Carmen is signed unless you wish to take the *circunvalación* to the western end of the resort).

[From Playa Blanca, drive north via Yaiza to Uga, then pursue route as described from Uga: to save time you may wish to omit Puerto del Carmen and simply remain on the GC 720 from Arrecife to Yaiza at the end of the route. 95 km/59 m: about 3½ hours without detours.]

[From Costa Teguise, bypass Arrecife and follow the GC 720 to Mácher, where you will join the route as described. At the end of the route, go straight over the Tahiche roundabout to re-enter Costa Teguise from the north. 70 km/44 m: 3 hours without detours.]

Route 2   The South

YAIZA – EL GOLFO – LOS HERVIDEROS –
JANUBIO – PLAYA BLANCA – PAPAGAYO

[83 km/51 miles – about two-and-a-half hours plus beach time]

From Puerto del Carmen, this route begins in the same way as route 1: that is, you leave Puerto del Carmen on the road for Mácher, where you turn left onto the GC 720 and cover familiar ground as far as Uga. This time, however, drive past Uga and continue to Yaiza.

Detour: Just before Uga an alternative route to the south coast presents itself, via the attractively situated village of Femés. If this appeals, leave the GC 720 about 6 km from Mácher and make a sharp clearly signposted left turn beside a particularly immaculate market garden with large 'Turk's cap' gateposts. This road climbs fairly steeply before emerging into a sandy valley, which by Lanzarotean standards has a distinctly pastoral air. Onions and peas are grown and there is grazing for goats.

A farm near Femés

Femés, which you reach after about 5 km, is spectacularly sited, perched on a natural balcony well above sea level with high hills on either side. Magnificent views down to Playa Blanca and across the strait of La Bocaina to Fuerteventura can be enjoyed from a viewpoint in front of the church. This church, dedicated to the patron saint of Lanzarote, San Marcial del Rubicón (Festival 7 July), is one of the oldest on the island, having been completed in 1733, and is built on the site of a still earlier church which was destroyed by English pirates in the sixteenth century. At one time it was an episcopal seat (of Bishop Pedro Manuel Davila y Cardenas, as a well-preserved inscription on the frontage tells us). Inside the church there is a collection of model sailing ships, but these can only be seen when the building is open for services. A well-kept plaza planted with Canary palms and geraniums flanks the church. There are a couple of restaurants in Femés and a shop selling Canarian crafts.

To the west of the church the Atalaya (look-out point) de Femés rises steeply to 608 metres – even better views are available from the summit if you fancy the walk. To the east a lower and much more easily climbed (ten minutes up) ridge offers a view of the valley, the Timanfaya mountains and a small part of the east coast.

Leaving Femés the road goes sharply downhill; a dramatic cliff soon appears on your right, a spur of the Atalaya in which the volcanic strata are clearly visible; quarrying has recently started here. Opposite, at a little under 1 km from Femés, what was once an extremely rough track off to the left has been widened and improved, though it remains unmetalled and unsignposted. This heads due south for about 5 km until it reaches a roundabout, where a left turn takes you to the Papagayo beaches and a right to Playa Blanca [15 km/9 m: 30 minutes or less]

Approaching Uga, watch out for the 'camels crossing' signs: there is a dromedary ranch just out of sight along the track on the left. Next you pass Uga's smoked salmon 'factory' and at the next roundabout drive straight on for Yaiza which, despite its having acquired two enormous roundabouts and a bypass in recent years, it would be a pity to miss.

Situated on the very edge of the lava fields, **Yaiza** wins the title of 'prettiest village in the Canaries' with monotonous regularity, and the inhabitants clearly take its reputation very seriously. Floral displays on red *picón* line the road at every entrance to the town, mature palm trees give welcome shade and there is scarcely a house that is not freshly decorated in the white and green Lanzarotean livery. It is well worth taking a short time to explore Yaiza: the central square, to your left as you drive through, makes a splendid setting for the large white church of Los Remedios (built in 1689 and restored in 1996). Inside the church, pillars of black lava support a painted timber roof. Behind it a few white streets invite a gentle stroll which will lead you to the justly popular Restaurant Jardines la Era, which specializes in authentic Canarian cuisine and is composed of

A doorway at Yaiza

a series of converted seventeenth-century farm buildings set in memorably delightful gardens. Another good restaurant in Yaiza, should you find yourself in the area around lunchtime, is El Volcán, a busy establishment on the main street. There are two art galleries, too, in the village: early evening is the best time to find them open.

From Yaiza continue on the GC 720, following signs to Playa Blanca past a large souvenir shop/bar complex where tourist coaches often stop. At the roundabout at the southern end of the village take the second exit (signed 'El Golfo'), which takes you under the bypass and through dramatic black fields of lava formed when the material ejected from the Timanfaya eruptions flowed down towards the sea. After 7 km there is a junction, where you bear right, descending steeply to the hamlet of Casas de El Golfo. There is a large car park to the left of the road before the village, from which it is only a short stroll to a viewpoint looking down over a small semi-circular bay in which the sea is divided by a bar of coarse black sand from a narrow lake of a quite extraordinary green colour (not unlike olivine!). **El Golfo,** as this lake is called, is in fact part of the crater of a volcano which was filled by the sea so long ago that the water in it is no longer very salty. It is, however, extremely deep, and the curious colour is said to be caused by the proliferation over centuries of micro-organisms which cloud the water as well as making it green. The lake lies at the bottom of a multi-coloured sandstone cliff, grotesquely striated, which is the half of the original crater rim which remains. The contrasting colours – gold, dark grey and red – make an unusual spectacle, which is much photographed. The view seaward is attractive also, with sandstone stacks and a small islet rising from the turquoise waters just off shore.*

Casas de El Golfo is a popular lunch spot with half a dozen restaurants, but is very quiet in the evenings. Returning up the hill from the village, carry straight on at the junction (signed 'Playa Blanca/Yaiza') to continue your circuit of the Montaña de El Golfo, reaching the coast once more at the far side. Now the road runs close to the sea

---

* Note that all this will change. At the time of preparing this edition the traditional, level approach to El Golfo, from the other end of the bay, was closed for restoration work and the construction of a new mirador within the cliff. When it is reopened, it will once again be possible to park on that side of the crater and walk into it along a path at the base of the cliff.

through black fields of lava. This area is a relatively 'new' part of Lanzarote, formed when lava from the Timanfaya eruptions met the sea and forced it back. The sea has never forgiven this encroachment, apparently, and all along this road waves beat ferociously against the lava, eroding it into strange shapes and breaking dramatically through rock arches and into caves. The most spectacular stretch of this coast is reached just after the very red Montaña Bermeja is passed on your left: this is the area known as '**Los Hervideros**' (literally 'the Boilings'). There is a car park off the road on the right, and a series of non-slippery walkways and steps has been skilfully constructed which enable you to view the many caves and blowholes from a safe vantage point.

Continuing south, there are further rock arches as you approach a large inlet, the **Laguna de Janubio** and its salt-pans – the last remaining on the island. There are plans for restoration work here and occasionally (but not as often as the postcards might suggest!) you may see men and women at work on the salt; but usually the pans are deserted, their squares of slightly different colours resembling a large chessboard. The Janubio pans only yield small quantities of brine today, used for canning, but in the years following World War Two 50,000 tons of salt was produced each year. The lagoon beyond the salt-pans attracts wild duck and other species of waterfowl and is popular with bird-watchers (and duck-shooters). On the seaward side of the lagoon there is a beach of fine black gravel pounded by the Atlantic waves. You may be tempted to join the inevitable sprinkling of people combing the beach in search of 'olivine', the greenish, transparent semi-precious stone (also known as peridot) which is much seen on Lanzarote. In fact small granules are relatively easy to spot among the caviar-like black stones, but if you like olivine there are usually men on the beach selling small containers of it, as well as trinkets made of larger pieces, for low prices.

The road runs around the back of the salt-pans where it reaches a roundabout: go straight on here (signed 'Las Breñas') then bear right for Playa Blanca on the new LZ 2. Faster and broader than the old road it supersedes (which still runs alongside, and which gives access to the southern end of the Janubio beach), this traverses a somewhat depressing area of unrelieved *malpaís* with views of the Ajaches mountain range to the left. After 9 km it reaches the south coast at the burgeoning resort of Playa Blanca.

Once a remote and pretty little fishing village with the ferry to Fuerteventura its only claim to fame, **Playa Blanca** is now a fully-fledged tourist resort. Hotels, shopping complexes and ever-expanding villa developments spread out from the harbour and beach, backed by an attractive promenade of bars and restaurants. The original beach, which gave the village its name, is now hopelessly inadequate for the number of visitors. In recent years, however, two new beaches have been constructed: to the west, Playa Flamingo is an appealing crescent of fine gold sand protected by moles and backed by rockeries which offers extremely safe bathing for families. On the other side of the old centre, Playa Dorada is larger and more exposed. The whole coastline between them has been landscaped and a long waterfront promenade binds the resort together.

A few kilometres to the east lie the **Papagayo** beaches, a string of half a dozen coves of pale gold sand which are among the finest in Spain. Not so long ago a secret paradise, the beaches have now been very definitely 'discovered'. Touristic development is creeping ever nearer to them and already reaches almost as far as the Punta del Águila where the Castillo de las Coloradas, a small watch-tower built in 1769, affords an excellent viewpoint. Along the coast east of Playa Blanca, new roads and roundabouts complete with street lamps are already in place, long before any houses are built (a Lanzarotean phenomenon also to be seen in Costa Teguise). But there is still no metalled road to the beaches and still hope that much discussed plans to conserve the area in some way before it sinks irretrievably beneath the tide of mass tourism will come to fruition.

The usual route to the beaches nowadays starts from the roundabout north of Playa Blanca, where a broad track brings you in due course to the first of the beaches, each as lovely as the next, though some are more exposed than others on windy days. There is no longer a village at Papagayo, though there was once; the only permanent structures in the area are a few bunkers built during the Second World War to protect the sea lanes to Fuerteventura.

All the beaches are sandy and gently shelving, and all face south or south-west; most of them are used by naturists, though these are very much in a minority. The fifth beach offers particularly good bathing and may be less crowded than those nearer to Playa Blanca. Note that there is no shade at any of the beaches. The distance from Playa Blanca is about 7 km and a minimum of an hour and a half should be allowed to see them. However, since this is essentially a trip in search of relaxation, most people will want to allow as much time as they can spare for them and will probably wish to return.

> *Detour*   Returning to Playa Blanca, a drive out to the Pechiguera lighthouse may be made by turning left at the petrol station (signposted 'Faro Pechiguera'). This takes you past the low Montaña Roja range, already the site of touristic development. At Pechiguera itself, a network of new roads under construction through the sandy scrubland is evidence that the lighthouse's years of lonely eminence are numbered: however, the new developments which threaten to engulf the area are not unattractive, pleasantly landscaped and uniformly built in modernised versions of Lanzarote's vernacular style. This is a windy spot, but the views of Fuerteventura are good. [10 km/6 m: 15–20 minutes]

Return to Puerto Del Carmen on the GC 720 via Yaiza and Uga, turning right to get back to the coast at Mácher; alternatively take the Papagayo track from the roundabout north of Playa Blanca, then head north to Femés at the next roundabout, as described in reverse at the beginning of this route.

[From Playa Blanca this is obviously an extremely short route; you can easily visit the beaches on another occasion, and may indeed have already done so. If you wish to follow the section of the route relating to Janubio and El Golfo, simply take the El Golfo exit from the roundabout south of Yaiza. 33 km/20 m: 2 hours]

[From Costa Teguise you must first drive round Arrecife on the circunvalación (bypass), then continue on the GC 720 past Tías to Mácher, where the route begins. 125 km/77 m: 3–4 hours]

Route 3   The North

TAHICHE – LOS VALLES – HARÍA –
MIRADOR DEL RÍO – CUEVA DE LOS
VERDES – JAMEOS DEL AGUA – GUATIZA –
COSTA TEGUISE

[96 km/60 miles – 4–5 hours allowing for stops at
Haría, Mirador del Río, Cueva de los Verdes and
Jameos del Agua, but excluding detours]

Much of the northern part of Lanzarote is green and pretty, with scenery that comes as a pleasant surprise if you have only seen the arid lands of the south so far. This route offers some magnificent views, so try to choose a clear day for it.

From Puerto del Carmen, take the Arrecife road and then the bypass, turning north off it onto the LZ 1 (signposted 'Lanzarote Norte, Orzola'). This will bring you to **Tahiche**, where the artist/architect César Manrique, who devoted much of his life to defending the dignity and charm of his homeland against the tidal wave of tourism, chose to make his home for many years. Manrique's magical split-level villa on the San Bartolomé road, the **Taro de Tahiche**, partly carved out of the lava and incorporating plants, water and natural rock formations, is now open to the public as the César Manrique Foundation, displaying works of art from Manrique's private collection (10.00–19.00 Mon-Fri, 10.00-14.00 Sats).

North of Tahiche, following signs for Teguise and Haría, the road passes the sprawling 'Oasis de Nazaret' urbaniza-tion: some of the more interesting villas are built into the hillside. The old hamlet of Nazaret with its tiny church lies to the left of the road. Drive past Teguise (see pp. 99–101) and Guanapay with its fortress north-east on the scenic GC 700. The road passes through undulating country, eventu-ally beginning to climb towards the large village of **Los Valles**. The soil here is of pale orange sand, and there are more trees and shrubs to be seen than in the south of the island – mostly palms and agave. After winter rain the land looks green. The Los Valles area was where many of the peasants made homeless by the Timanfaya eruptions settled, taking with them the contents of their church of

Santa Catalina and building a new church dedicated to the saint in memory of their devastated homelands.

At that time largely uncultivated, the area has been transformed by the refugees into a fertile agricultural landscape, where crops grow well. Vegetables flourish in terraces built up the sides of the valley with very uniform dry-stone walls. A few vines grow here, too, ingeniously grafted on to prickly pears which have greater water retention. You are sure to see people working in the fields, the men in felt hats ('*chapeos*'), the women wearing Canarian headgear: straw hats with a black ribbon for wives and widows, and white bonnets for single women. The onion harvest in February is a particularly busy time, when whole families can be seen at work. The lack of agricultural machinery is most noticeable, as elsewhere on Lanzarote, and ploughing with a donkey or camel (or even both!) is a not uncommon sight.

After Los Valles, the road climbs steeply, through a deep cutting. At the highest point it often becomes very windy, but the views in all directions are spectacular. The hills of the northern part of the island attract clouds, and the resulting moisture produces a glorious carpet of poppies and other wild flowers in winter and spring. At the top of the ridge you are higher than Guanapay and can see over it to Fuerteventura and the mountains of the south. A few minutes on from Los Valles the entrance to the **Parque Eólico** (Wind Farm, see p. 30) comes up on the right, while ahead the military communications equipment on the summit of Peñas del Chache comes into view.

Detour: Immediately after the wind farm a recently improved minor road to the left is signposted 'Las Nieves'. You may have noticed the little white hermitage to which this road leads from various points along the route; it can in fact be seen from many parts of the island. It is a tranquil spot, and one of our favourites on Lanzarote. The hermitage itself is pretty and surrounded by colourful planting. A sandy area a few yards before it on the road is a magnificent viewpoint, giving an almost aerial view of the beach of Famara, the flat plain of El Jable and the desert of Sóo. At this point, early in the year, the arid ground is studded with masses of tiny mauve squills. This road is very little used and one can usually enjoy the views in complete solitude, poised between sea and sky. This exhilarating site has seen regular protests lately, against the army's building of a barracks near the church: Manrique had plans for a second mirador here but the ideas produced for this by a younger designer have so far not found favour with the authorities or conservationist group El Guincho, which also questions the need for another attraction so near to the Mirador del Río. [5 km/3.5 m: 20 minutes]

Return to the main road, which now drops slightly and becomes a corniche above two valleys: to the right is that of Tabayesco, with views down to Arrieta on the east coast with the lonely Roque del Este beyond; and straight ahead lies the so-called 'valley of 1,000 palms'. This is the valley of Haría, a green and fertile region where the contrast to the barren rockiness of the southern part of Lanzarote could not be more marked. The road winds steeply down into the valley, its verges covered with wild flowers at certain times of year, including *Ferula lancerottensis*, a giant fennel unique to the island. It offers a couple of places to stop and admire the extensive views.

At the first, a bar/restaurant called Los Helechos has been built offering panoramic views from its large dining room; it is popular with coach parties. There is a little shop here, as also at the smaller Mirador ('Viewpoint') de Haría establishment a couple of turns further down the road. The

Palm trees at Haría

Traditional pottery

view from here is perhaps the better of the two, with the town of Haría visible: also the mirador is a natural rock garden and very pretty in itself. Bright green lizards dart in and out of magnificent clumps of creamy yellow wild chrysanthemums which cling to the steep cliffs.

The valley of the palms at Haría does indeed have the air of an oasis. Visitors are told a legend to the effect that each palm tree celebrates the birth of a baby girl in the town, but it is more likely that most of the trees represent the remains of a large palm grove planted in the sixteenth century. **Haría** itself is the municipal capital of the northern part of the island, a prosperous and dignified community whose sheltered position has always brought it success in agriculture. Bougainvillea drips over the quiet streets, and to your left as you enter the town is the Taller de Artesanía where potters, basket-weavers, wood-carvers and embroiderers can be seen at work and their wares purchased (Tues–Fri 10.30–13.00 and 16.00–18.30, Mon and Sat 10.30–13.00). Opposite, Per Eckhoff's shop sells craftwork, cacti and bonsai, marmalade from local oranges and a very reasonably priced fruity red wine. A new attraction that visitors may find surprising, in this reserved and dignified little town, is the Almogarem Museum of Miniatures, situated beside the large car park at the entrance to Haría (admission 500 ptas, children 250): it displays curiosities such as a bullfight scene painted on a pinhead, a football match on a grain of rice and preserved fleas arrayed in traditional Mexican dress! Mule rides are also on offer here, which take you on a (very) brief tour of the town for 700 ptas (children 500 ptas). In the centre the modern church, with a Museum of Sacred Imagery next door (open 11.00–13.00, 16.00–18.00 Mon--Fri) stands in the Plaza León y Castillo shaded by mature eucalyptus trees – a welcome place to sit in hot weather and sip a cool drink at the Papa Loca bar nearby.

The valley of Haría culminates in the deceptively serene table-like bulk of Monte Corona. Deceptive because this volcano erupted violently in ancient times and was responsible for the *malpaís* (literally, 'badlands') that cover the north-eastern part of the island to this day. (By contrast the southern slopes of the mountain are partially cultivated.) North of Haría, the road passes Las Cascadas restaurant, a favourite lunch spot for coach parties, before curving sharply left (signed 'Mirador del Río/Guinate') to enter Máguez. A sign 2 km further on directs you to one of Lanzarote's newer attractions, the **Guinate Tropical Park**. Here there are aviaries displaying 300 rare and exotic birds, as well as gamebirds, pigeons and all kinds of poultry; small exotic mammals such as meerkats and wallabies are also featured. Too many of the birds are caged and seem to lack companionship, but the park is popular with children (open 10.00–17.00 daily, admission 1000 ptas, children 500 ptas). A display featuring performing parrots is held six times a day (at 11.30, and thereafter hourly on the half hour). Beyond the park the road terminates near to the jagged end of the Riscos de Famara, with stunning views of La Graciosa and the other offshore islands. (Back on the main road, exciting views of both sides of Lanzarote from a higher point than this can be seen by walking or driving a circuit of farm tracks signed 'Camino de Guatifay' a little beyond the Guinate turn-off.)

The main road skirts Monte Corona (the energetic can scramble up to the lip of the crater) to reach **Ye**. This village (its rather odd name means 'the end of the earth' in the Guanche language) is famous for its wrestlers and originally owed its existence to the dye industry. In Roman times Lanzarote, Fuerteventura and their satellite islets were known as the 'Purpurariae' in reference to the purple dye obtained from the lichen *orchilla* which grew on the rocks, and Ye was a centre for its extraction.

At the far end of the village a sharp left turn is signposted 'Mirador del Río'. The crown-shaped rim of Monte

Corona's crater is seen very clearly from here on your right, looking considerably more forbidding than it did from the south. A further 2 km brings you to the Mirador, which was formerly the site of a gun battery (the Batería del Río) protecting Lanzarote's northern approaches. (The cannon removed from here are now displayed outside the Castillo de San Gabriel in Arrecife.) The Mirador itself is a large domed crescent-shaped building covered in small lava blocks and cunningly designed by César Manrique so that it appears merely to be a mound that is integral with the cliff. Park in the large car park and enter the discreet doorway in a large convex lava-block wall (entrance fee 350 ptas). From here a curving whitewashed tunnel with alcoves containing peasant-style pottery leads to the restaurant and viewing room. This is semi-circular, with huge rounded plexi-glass windows looking out onto a view that is genuinely spectacular. The immense height of the cliff on which the Mirador rests (some 480 metres) allows the visitor to look down, as if from an aircraft, on to the island of La Graciosa and the narrow channel (El Río) which separates it from Lanzarote. Beyond the windows is a small balcony with telescopes. La Graciosa, a pale barren island with two small villages, four hills and magnificent white beaches, is spread out like a map; beyond it you have good views of Montaña Clara and Alegranza, the two uninhabited minor islands. The range of

The interior of the Mirador del Río

blues and greens in the waters of El Río is stunning, and a further, rather incongruous colour is part of the scene: directly below, on the Lanzarotean shore, are the salt-pans of Salinas del Río, one of which is a strange strawberry pink.

The interior of the restaurant at the Mirador del Río is a work of art in itself: the walls and ceiling are moulded in white curves and from the twin domes of the ceiling are suspended two immense metal cascades sculpted by Manrique. Upstairs there is a small shop selling local handicrafts and higher still a rooftop viewing platform. The Mirador is open between 10.00 and 18.45 daily.

Back in Ye, turn left to leave the village and enter the region known as the *malpaís* de Corona. Thousands of years older than the lava fields around Timanfaya, this area is slightly less black: spurges and succulents manage to cling to it, and some cultivation is possible. The mansion on the hillside to your right is the Torrecilla (Fortress) de Domingo.

> *Detour:* Three km from Ye on the GC 710 there is a left turn signposted 'Orzola' at the small village of Los Molinos, on which one can make a pleasant detour to take a closer look at the north-eastern corner of Lanzarote. A quiet minor road runs down to the coast with views out to sea and the Roque del Este. The countryside by the road is still the '*malpaís* de Corona', though some vines, figs and prickly pears grow in tiny walled fields. **Órzola** is the small fishing port from which ferries to La Graciosa sail (see p. 80), an attractive town on a very exposed coast where the north-east winds blow straight into the little harbour. At the approach to the village is the Pardela Natural Park (open 10.00–16.00 every day), a 'recreational farm' where examples of the indigenous flora and fauna can be seen as well as traditional crafts. A small pedestrian promenade extends eastwards from Órzola harbour, and westwards one can wander into the rough ground between the village and the hills to get further views of the cliffs on which the Mirador del Río stands, and of a large sandstone stack 20 metres high off Punta Fariones. There are several restaurants in Órzola, all serving fresh fish.
>
> From here take the coast road south-east. Bordering the *malpaís* there is a series of startlingly white little beaches, sometimes dotted with contrasting black lava,

where the waves drive in over a series of small reefs to create turquoise pools – Charca de la Laja, Caletón Blanco and Caleta del Mojón Blanco. Their existence is due to sand blowing over from the Sahara, 112 kilometres to the east; all are quiet and make tempting stopping places for a picnic or a swim. South of this attractive string of beaches, the road cuts through the worst of the *malpaís*: dark brown lava fields where even after 6,000 years very little grows. Nine km south of Órzola, turn right and shortly afterwards the sign for the Cueva de los Verdes appears on the left, where the main route is rejoined. [16 km/10 m: 30–40 minutes]

From Ye the GC 710 continues to descend through the *malpaís* with views of the east coast and the Roque del Este out to sea. Six km after Ye a narrow road with passing places (signposted 'Cueva de los Verdes/Jameos del Agua') goes off to the left. Take this and after 2 km you will reach the **Cueva de los Verdes** (large car parks on the left of the road).

One of the many natural wonders on Lanzarote, these caves are part of a 'volcanic tube' some 6 km long and extending out to sea. Molten lava from the Monte Corona eruption formed a river here, of which the outer edges cooled and hardened while the core continued hot and flowing – hence the tube. Being of volcanic origin the caves are not damp and dripping (there are no stalagmites and stalactites). They have been simply lit by Jesús Soto Morales, of Fuerteventura, and a guide takes parties of about 50 people at a time for a slightly strenuous walk, involving some ducking and scrambling, of about 2 km (price 700 ptas). The caves consist of four separate levels of which only the first (lowest) and third are negotiable. The shapes and colours of the various lava strata are weird and interesting. You climb rock stairways and squeeze through narrow passageways to reach a large chamber known as El Refugio where a small auditorium for concerts has been made (in fact concerts here are fairly rare, due to the difficulty of manoeuvring the instruments into the caves). It was in El Refugio that the early population of Lanzarote regularly used to hide from pirates and other invaders. The temperature inside the caves remains at a constant 18°C throughout the year. A memorable feature of the tour is an optical illusion so startling that it would be a pity to disclose it (guided tours at least hourly on the hour, 10.00–18.00 daily).

Turn right towards the coast after leaving the Cueva, and a few hundred metres will bring you to a crossroads; go straight over this to visit another section of the same lava tunnel, the famous **Jameos del Agua**. This segment, some 730 feet long, is very different, for here César Manrique's artistic hand has been at work enhancing the natural beauty. The grotto at Jameos del Agua is Manrique's masterwork on Lanzarote and has become the island's major showpiece. Park near the sea and, passing a small circular shop built of lava, enter the cave down a steep flight of steps, which bring you to a level area where there is an attractively laid-out bar: further steps lead down to the cave itself – which is really more of a grotto, containing as it does a deep pool of clear water beneath a high rock ceiling under which birds twitter and from which massive plants are suspended. The water in the pool has filtered through layers of rock from the sea, becoming desalinated in the process, and is the home of a small white crab (*Munidopsis polymorpha*), almost entirely blind, whose natural home is 3000 metres below the sea. Presumably its ancestors were trapped here by the geological upheaval thousands of years ago. Despite the presence of large quantities of small change in the water (the curiously universal urge to throw money into the pool is now expressly forbidden as the corrosion affects the crabs),

Jameos del Agua

it is quite easy to pick out these tiny creatures when you have got your eye in.

A path along the side of the lake brings you to a tiered area open to the air, formed when part of the roof of the cave collapsed. Here plant life is rampant, and attractively designed staircases lead in all directions to a succession of bars and picturesque corners. There is also a dance floor at this end of the cave. Beyond the area of seating one emerges into full sunlight at the highest level where there is a pleasantly irregular swimming pool with more plants and tastefully arranged rock formations everywhere. The turquoise of the water, the dazzling white surround and the exotic profusion of plants and flowers will have you fumbling for your camera! Further on there is a 550-seat concert auditorium, more galleries and seating areas for functions, with porthole windows looking onto the *malpaís*. Back at ground level is the Casa de Volcanes, housing geological displays. There is also a small beach at Jameos del Agua, which most visitors do not find.

Jameos del Agua is open daily from 09.30–18.45 (admission 800 ptas), and on Tuesdays, Fridays and Saturdays also from 19.00 p.m. to 00.30 a.m. (admission 1100 ptas), when it functions as a night club with dancing and often displays of Canarian folk dancing, etc.

A fascinating aspect of the caves that you are unlikely to see (since it has only been explored by a handful of divers) is the so-called Atlántida Tunnel which is the continuation of the volcanic tube from Jameos del Agua out under the sea bed to a depth of 64 metres. The 1.6-km tunnel is of enormous dimensions, often over 12 metres high and almost as wide, and it twists and turns from a small entrance which is actually in the Jameos pool.

From Jameos del Agua the coast road continues southwards past the growing fishing village of Punta Mujeres, reaching the main road (GC 710) just before the small port of **Arrieta**. Tourism has made little impact here, but there is a handful of good fish restaurants and a fine beach, Playa de la Garita, which has seen recent refurbishment. At the roundabout outside the village follow signs for Arrecife/ Teguise. From here onwards you are once again on a good, fast road, which next brings you to the unusual cochineal region of Lanzarote, centring on the towns of Mala and Guatiza. The process of harvesting this natural dye from the cochineal insect is described on pp. 59–60: as you enter

Mala you will begin to see the fields of cactus on which they feed on both sides of the road. You may like to stop and examine a few to see if you can spot the white powdery patches which indicate the beetles' presence.

A couple of kilometres further on, the surrounding fields still full of cochineal cactus, you come to **Guatiza**, a compact, prosperous-looking town with a eucalyptus avenue, a church of distinguished simplicity and a prominent windmill. Just beyond the latter is César Manrique's last creation (opened in March 1990), the **Jardín de Cactus**, its car park dominated by a huge metal cactus some 7m high. Below the windmill (now used to grind *gofio* for sale in small quantities to tourists), Manrique created a characteristic amphitheatre of black lava terraces, in which grow some 4000 varieties of cacti and succulents, their architectural shapes complemented by statuesque outcrops of rock. The park is open daily from 10.00–18.45 (admission 425 ptas), and there is a snack bar and a shop. From Guatiza the road takes you swiftly back towards Tahiche through hilly country – a good area for walking. The northern entrance to Costa Teguise (in the form of a white plaster archway) comes up on your left after some 6 km, and if time permits you may like to take the opportunity to have a look at this development which lies about 5 km to the south-east. (Otherwise carry straight on to Tahiche, where a left turn will take you back to the Arrecife *circunvalación* and home.)

The Jardín de Cactus, Guatiza

Costa Teguise is perhaps Lanzarote's smartest area of tourist development, and, enthusiasts will tell you, its most fashionable: the Spanish royal family have a holiday home here, Las Maretas, a villa which previously belonged to King Hussein of Jordan. The whole area, once largely devoted to salt-pans, was owned by the Rio Tinto Zinc Corporation and development permission was granted on the understanding that building would be limited, and of sympathetic design: initially César Manrique was involved as a consultant. Since then, however, the development has been acquired by ERCROS, a division of the Spanish arm of the Kuwaiti investment office, and many lovers of Lanzarote feel that these original commitments have been to some extent abandoned. The result is a somewhat over-extended resort; many of the larger buildings ape international clichés, there is less effort to reflect traditional Lanzarotean style than elsewhere on the island, and residents seem to spend a great deal of time driving from one section of the resort to another. On the plus side, Costa Teguise offers comfortable accommodation, some excellent restaurants and a lively nightlife scene.

Costa Teguise has five beaches: Playa del Ancla is very small, east-facing and rocky in parts, but offers safe bathing; Playa Bastián is rocky at the water's edge with a strong current; Playa del Jablillo, sheltered by a breakwater, provides safe bathing in shallow water; Playa de las Cucharas, the largest beach, is open and windswept and the resort's main watersports centre; most northerly, Playa de los Charcos, backed by the Lanzarote Beach Club, is protected by sea walls and a natural reef. The showpiece of the resort of the 5-star *gran lujo* Meliá Salinas Hotel, still the most luxurious on Lanzarote, whose opening in 1977 provided the initial spark for development on this coast. It features a spectacular central atrium, consisting of a large water garden with waterfalls and exotic plants including full grown trees: little paths lead in and out of this 'jungle' and further plants drip down from the floors above.

There are now three other large hotels and around fifty villa and apartment complexes in the resort, and new shops and restaurants are opening all the time. Sports facilities (including Lanzarote's only golf course, see p. 72) are excellent, with a wide range of watersports available (especially at Playa de las Cucharas) and the Acualanza water park catering particularly for families.

Leave Costa Teguise by the south-western exit (at right angles to the road on which you came in). This will bring you to the Arrecife *circunvalación*, where you should turn right and remain on the bypass (following 'Aeropuerto' signs) until you have gone right round Arrecife. The road to Puerto del Carmen is signposted shortly after passing the airport turn-off.

[From Playa Blanca the route as set out here is probably too long for comfort: either it entails a very early start and late return to your home base or some judicious cutting should be done – perhaps the detour round Orzola and the excursion down to Costa Teguise. We do recommend you to try to see something of the north of the island, though; it is so refreshingly different from the landscapes you will have become accustomed to at the other extremity. To start the route, go through Yaiza, turn left at Uga and head towards Teguise via La Geria and the Campesino Monument; at Teguise pick up the GC 700 road to Los Valles and follow the route as described on p.110. After passing through Guatiza make for Tahiche, where a left turn will take you down to the Arrecife bypass and home on the GC 720 via Tías, Mácher and Uga. 147 km/91 m: 7 hours minimum, including lunching time and visits.]

[From Costa Teguise, leave the resort via the golf course, which will bring you to the Taro de Tahiche roundabout. Here turn right for Teguise and the start of the route. 70 km/43m: about 4 hours]

INDEX

agriculture 43–4, 47, 55, 56–7, *57*, 79, *94*, 95, 110
Águilar, Ildefonso 64, 66
airlines 4
airport (Aeropuerto de Lanzarote) situated alongside Playa de Guasimeta between Arrecife and Puerto del Carmen; original terminal building designed by César Manrique incorporates his murals and ceiling draped with green and white awnings; expansion plans due to be completed in 1998 4–5, 10, *11*, 26
Ajaches, Los mountain range in S of island 33, 34–5, 93, 102, 107
Alegranza most northerly island of the Canary archipelago, rising to 289m; uninhabited; lighthouse on most easterly point; puffin colony 45, 81, 97, 115
'Angel Guerra' 101
animals 42–4
aquarium 82
Arabs 50
Arrecife (pop. 38,439) Lanzarote's capital is home to almost half the island's population; a bustling, unpretentious town with a traffic problem, an excellent harbour, pleasant seafront promenade and good beaches close at hand 4, 5, 6, 7, 9, 10, 11, 12, 14–15, 18, 19, 25, 26, 27, 28, 29, 30, 38, 40, 41, 44, 45, 50, 53, 54, 55, 57, 58, 59, 61, 62, 63–4, 65, 66, 67, 68, 71, 72, 73, 74, 76, 83, 84, **90–2**, 102, 115, 121, 122

Arrieta small E coast fishing village, little affected by tourism despite its proximity to Jameos del Agua; a good beach, Playa de la Garita, connected to the village by a bridge, several fish restaurants, 19, 40, 67, 74, 76, **119–20**
art galleries 62, 63–5, 92, 102, 106, 110
Atalaya de Femés peak (608 m) W of Femés 34, 104
Atlántida Tunnel volcanic 'tube' formed by molten lava flowing from Monte Corona and extending for 6 km; Cueva de los Verdes and Jameos del Agua are both sections of the tunnel 34, 119
Azores 33, 37

Baeza, Juan de 53
bananas 17, 18, 57
banks 26, 91
Barreto, Dr José María 65
bars 24, 25
beaches 2, 3, 74, 92, 93, 98, 107, 108, 115, 117, 119, 121
Berbers 47, 90
Betancuria (Fuerteventura) 79–80
Bethancourt, Jean de 50, 51, 52, 53, 79
Bethancourt, Maciot de 52, 81, 99
Biosphere Reserve 3, 38
birds 38, 44–5, 59, 81, 82, 91, 107, 114
boat trips 77
Bocaina, La shallow channel dividing Lanzarote from Isla de Lobos and Fuerteventura; approx 9 km. wide and only

The church of San Ginés, Arrecife

about 100 m. deep 33
books 69, 91
breakdown services 8
Breñas, Las flowery village
spreading along a ridge N of
Playa Blanca; church of San
Luís Gonzaga 67
Brito, Juan 65, 69
buses 5, 10
butterflies 2, 45–6

Cabrera Felipe, Blas 65, 92
Cactus Garden *see* Jardín de
Cactus

Cádiz 5, 6, 51
Caleta de Famara, La 20, 40,
42, 61, 98, *see also* Playa de
Famara
Caleta del Mojón Blanco
pale gold beach at NE tip of
Lanzarote, backed by the
malpaís de Corona 117
Caleta del Sebo chief village
on La Graciosa; sheltered
fishing harbour, impressive
view of the cliffs of NW
Lanzarote across the strait of
El Río 15, 81

Caletón Blanco popular white sandy beach SE of Órzola; rather exposed to wind 117

camels *see* dromedaries

camping 15

Canarian Gazette 30, 32

car hire 5, 7, 8–9, 79, 85

carnival 67

Carthaginians 49

Casa Museo del Campesino 65, 68

Casas de El Golfo hamlet N of El Golfo; fish restaurants 20, 106

casino 25

Castillo de Guanapay 16th-century fortress overlooking Teguise, now housing the Museo del Emigrante Canario 53, 65, 101

Castillo de las Coloradas fortress on S coast, E of Playa Blanca 51, 108

Castillo de San Gabriel fortress on Arrecife waterfront, housing archaeological museum 53, 65, 91–2, 115

Castillo de San José fort built 1771–79 on a promontory N of Arrecife on the orders of Charles III, largely in order to provide work for the indigent islanders (whence it became known as the 'Starvation Fortress'). Abandoned in 1890s, and restored in 1969 by Manrique to house International Museum of Modern Art, with recital room and panoramic bar/restaurant 19, 29, 46, 62, 63, *64*, 66

Castillo de Santa Bárbara *see* Castillo de Guanapay

Castillo del Rubicón 51, 53 *see also* Castillo de las Coloradas

Charca de la Laja small golden sandy beach SE of Órzola, sheltered from north winds 117

Charco de Los Clicos *see* El Golfo

Charles III 63

cheese 17

children's activities 82

Chinijo archipelago collection of islets off NW tip of Lanzarote; La Graciosa is the largest island of the group and the only inhabited one

churches 52, *78*, 91, 96, 99–100, 104, 105

Clavijo y Fajardo, José 101

climate 1, 36–7

clinics 28–9

Club La Santa sports village on W coast near Tinajo 70, 71, 75, 76

coach trips 77–8

cochineal 59–60, 119–20

concerts 66

Constitution of Cádiz 55

consulates 31

Corralejo (Fuerteventura) 6, 78, 79

Costa Teguise formerly an area of salt-flats N of Arrecife, but now Lanzarote's second largest resort, with a population set to rise to 20,000 by 2002; five beaches, golf course, water park, excellent sporting facilities 1, 9, 10, 11, 12, 14, 18, 20, 24, 26, 27, 28, 29, 31, 32, 56, 59, 63, 67, 68, 70, 71, 72, 74, 75, 82, 85, **121–2**

crafts 65, 68–9, 83, 96, 101, 113, *113*

credit cards 26, 28

cruise liners 6

Cueva de los Verdes spectacular caves in a section of the 'volcanic tube' formed by the eruption of Monte Corona in NE Lanzarote before recorded history; now

individual plants are grown in a deep cavity which is then partially filled with porous volcanic ash granules and protected from the prevailing wind by a semi-circular wall of lava blocks; vines are the main crop and the region's famous *malvasía* is a strong and characterful wine that amply justifies the labour involved in producing it 7, 18, *57*, 66, 73, 77, **95–6**

gofio 16, 47, 65

golf 72, 122

Gomera, La 52

Graciosa, La largest of the minor islands (Chinijo Archipelago) off Lanzarote and the only inhabited one (pop. 600). Most of the inhabitants live in Caleta del Sebo, but there is a second tiny settlement, Pedro Barba, to the east; they live almost exclusively from fishing; reached by ferry from Órzola, La Graciosa has several fine beaches, the largest of which is Playa de las Conchas on the NW side of the island 15, 42, 45, 53–4, 67, 71, 74, 77, **80–2**, 115, 116

Gran Canaria 17, 55

Gran Tarajal (Fuerteventura) 79

Grifo, El 18, 97

Guadarfía 50, 51, 52, 99

Guanapay 53, 101–2

Guanarame 50

Guanches 16, 17, 47–9, 51, 54, 69, 76

Guatiza with Mala, the centre of Lanzarote's waning cochineal industry in the NE of the island; elegant church of S Cristo de las Aguas and site of Jardin de Cactus (*qv*) 59, *60*, 62, 68, 119, **120**, *120*

Güime pretty village sprawling .

down the hillside above the busy Arrecife-Tías road; rarely visited by foreigners, Güime remains a quiet and typically Canarian community 67, 83

Guinate Tropical Park 82, 114

Guincho, El 38, 112

gyms 13, 70–1

Hacha Grande 35

Haría (pop. 3378) capital of the northern municipality and famous for its surrounding forest of palms; quiet and dignified village chosen by César Manrique as his last home and burial place 11, 21, 38, 39, 40, 41, 42, 56, 63, 66, 67, 68, 77, 78, 83, 112, *112*, **113–14**

Hawkins, Sir John 53

health care 28–9

Herrera, Diego de 52

Herrera y Rochas, Agustín de 43, 52–3

Hervideros, Los area of rock arches and blowholes on SW coast 36, *48*, **107**

Hierro 52

horse riding *see* riding

hospital 71

hostales 13

hotels 12–15, 80, 121

Hussein, King 121

Ibañez, Luis 1, 4, 23, 74

Ico 59

ICONA 75

industry 58–60

insects 45–6

insurance 8

Isleta, La circular islet opposite the lagoon at Club La Santa (*qv*)

Islote de Hilario central area in Timanfaya National Park, site of restaurant and starting point for coach tours of the volcanic route 35, *35*, 40, 62, 87–8, 89

Jable, El sandy plain, E of Muñique and Sóo, which forms the central section of the island, linking the northern and southern mountain ranges

Jameos del Agua section of the same volcanic tube as Cueva de los Verdes, with a partially collapsed roof and seawater pool which is home to a small albino crab. The Jameos ('Cavern') was converted by César Manrique in 1966 to form an unusually beautiful night club cum entertainment area, with bars, dance floor, gardens, pools and a magnificent auditorium 10, 25, *25*, 34, 39, 44, 46, 61–2, 66, 78, **118–19**, *118*

Janubio formerly the most important salt-pans in Lanzarote, these *salinas* in the SW of the island have ceased production, but are to be restored and preserved as an outdoor museum; the lagoon beyond attracts wild duck and other waterfowl, while the Playa de Janubio nearby is composed of fine black gravel mingled with small fragments of the semi-precious olivine (peridot) which features in much of the locally made jewellery 58, *58*, **107**

Jardín de Cactus 62, **120**, *120*
Juan II 81
Juba II 49

karting 73

La Salle, Gadifer de 50, 51, 52, 80

Lancelot 30, 32
Las Palmas 1, 4, 5, 6, 12, 31, 55, 91
lavatories 29
Lobos, Isla de small island off Fuerteventura in La Bocaina strait; a single small peak (122 m.) dwindles gradually, like a dragon's tail, into the sea. The name translates as 'seals' (not wolves!): Gadifer de la Salle, first conqueror of Lanzarote, took a small party over to Lobos to hunt the seals for shoe leather soon after his arrival, but during his absence his troops on Lanzarote mutinied and de la Salle is said to have been compelled to live on the abundant seal meat for several weeks before he was able to escape. Today Lobos is inhabited solely by the lighthouse keeper and his family, but the island, which offers excellent swimming and snorkelling and forms part of the National Park which includes the dunes on Fuerteventura can be visited twice daily from that island or (less easily) from Lanzarote 33, 43, 71, 77, 79, **80**, 93

Los Valles sprawling village N of Teguise in an upland valley made fertile after many of the peasants rendered homeless by the 1730s eruptions elected to settle here; properly Los Valles de Santa Catalina (after Santa Catalina, one of the villages destroyed in the eruption); laboriously terraced fields, still farmed by traditional methods, cover the hillside; the island's largest wind farm (Parque Eólico) is nearby 30,

55, 62, 66, 67, **110–11**

Mácher village lying alongside the main road on the hillside above the western end of Puerto del Carmen; low houses with orderly vegetable gardens with windbreaks made of boxes or straw; nowadays most of the population works in the tourist centres on the coast 21, 67, 93

Máguez village N of Haría; Manrique mural behind the altar in the church 67, 68, 114

Mala contiguous with Guatiza and, like its sister village, originally dependent on the cochineal industry; small beach (Playa del Seifio) and, to the west of Presa (Dam) de Mala forms a small reservoir which can be reached on foot by a path which eventually leads to Teguise 59, 67, 119, 120

Malocello, Lancelotto 50

malpaís **de Corona** 34, 91, 114, 116

malvasía 18, 56, 96, 97

Mancha Blanca prosperous agricultural village on N extremity of Timanfaya National Park. It is here that the Virgin of the Sorrows is said to have appeared and commanded the lava flow from the Tinguatón eruptions of 1824 to cease – the Ermita (Hermitage) de la Virgen de los Dolores commemorates the event, and is the site of the notable pilgrimage (*romería*) and Fiesta of the Virgin of the Volcanoes on 15 September 36, 67, 68, 89, 96

Manrique Cabrera, César 2, 4, 20, 22, 23, 26, 56, 61–3, 64, 87, 90, 92, 97, 98, 102, 110, 115, 118, 120, 121

maps 9

markets 68, 69, 78, 91, 99

Masdache wine-producing village at eastern extremity of La Geria 18, 39

Matagorda formerly 'Las Salinas de Matagorda', an area of salt pans, this beach resort lies north of Playa de los Pocillos, itself a 'suburb' of Puerto del Carmen; good windsurfing, but beach lies under the flightpath into Lanzarote airport, so can be noisy 59, 75, 102

medical services 13, 14, 15, 28–9

mineral water 18, 30

Mirador del Río former gun battery overlooking El Río and the island of La Graciosa, transformed by César Manrique into a stunning viewing area; almost completely camouflaged within the cliff, the building incorporates a snack bar and shop 39, 62, 74, 77, 78, **115–16**, *115*

Montaña Blanca sizeable agricultural village equidistant from San Bartolomé, Masdache and Tao; colourful mobile on roundabout outside the village 67

Montaña Clara small uninhabited islet off the NW tip of La Graciosa; central peak 256 m high 45, 81, 115

Montañas del Fuego *see* Timanfaya National Park

Monte Corona ancient volcano in N of island, whose lava stream forms the *malpaís* de Corona; the Atlántida tunnel (*qv*) extends 6 km to

of Teguise, backed by spectacular Riscos (Cliffs) de Famara; faces directly into prevailing winds with large Atlantic rollers which make the beach popular with surfers and windsurfers but often dangerous for swimmers; César Manrique spent much of his childhood in the small village at the W end of the beach, La Caleta de Famara (*qv*) 20, 61, 74, 75, 76, 78, 98

Playa de Guasimeta sandy beach alongside Lanzarote airport 4

Playa de Janubio 74 *see also* Janubio

Playa de la Arena beach of dark sand at Playa Quemada (*qv*)

Playa de la Garita 119 *see also* Arrieta

Playa de Las Conchas glorious golden sandy beach on NW coast of La Graciosa 74, 81

Playa de las Cucharas longest beach in Costa Teguise (*qv*); Blue Flag, golden sand, watersports 71, 75, 76, 121

Playa de los Charcos artificial beach in Costa Teguise (*qv*) backed by Lanzarote Beach Club; Blue Flag, protected by sea walls and natural reef 75, 121

Playa de los Pocillos beach resort N of (and contiguous with) Puerto del Carmen; vast beach (Blue Flag), with recreation park under construction 24, 32, 71, 75, 102

Playa del Ancla small east-facing beach at southern extremity of Costa Teguise resort 121

Playa del Cable beach between Arrecife and Playa Honda 92

Playa del Jablillo small, sheltered sandy beach in Costa Teguise (*qv*); Blue Flag, safe bathing 121

Playa del Reducto 92

Playa Dorada artificially constructed beach E of Playa Blanca; water sports, Blue Flag 75, 108

Playa Flamingo man-made beach and lagoon SW of Playa Blanca 25, 108

Playa Honda prosperous residential development to W of Arrecife, built alongside safe bathing beach directly to E of the airport 74, 102

Playa Quemada literally 'burnt beach'; quiet hamlet S of Puerto del Carmen; fishing and scuba diving 43, 71, 73, 74, 93

Pliny the Elder 49

police 7, 8, 32

population 53, 55

Portugal 50, 52

postal services 27–8

potatoes 16–17, 56

pottery 47, 65, 68–9, 83, *113*

property purchase 32

Ptolemy 49

public holidays 27, 59, 67–8 *see also fiestas*

Puerto Calero purpose-built yacht resort S of Puerto del Carmen 22, 64, 70, 71, 72, 76, 93

Puerto de los Marmoles main harbour of Arrecife 91

Puerto del Carmen Lanzarote's senior and largest resort, accommodating some 60 per cent of the island's visitors; Puerto del Carmen grew from the small fishing port of La Tiñosa at the W end of the modern resort:

here, in the 'Old Town', can be found the church, the small original harbour and a huddle of older dwellings and warehouses, many of them now restaurants; the long sandy beach to the E has been awarded a Blue Flag; behind it, bars, discos, shops, car hire offices and over 100 restaurants spread along the 6-km seafront road; good sporting facilities, lively nightlife 1, *3*, 6, 7, 9, 10, 12, 13, *13*, 18, 22, 24, *24*, 26, 27, 28, 31, 56, 63, 64, 67, 68, 69, 70, 71, 72, 74, 75, 76, 77, 82, 85, 93

Puerto del Rosario (Fuerteventura) 80

Puerto Naos fishing harbour of Arrecife 25, 91–2

Punta del Águila headland between Playa Blanca and Papagayo beaches, crowned by Castillo de las Coloradas (*qv*) 108

Punta del Papagayo most southerly point on Lanzarote

Punta del Sordo cape E of Órzola; Lanzarote's most northerly point

Punta Mujeres small fishing harbour N of Arrieta; black beach and limited tourist accommodation 119

Punta Pechiguera SW extremity of Lanzarote, where a pencil-thin lighthouse protects the channel between Lanzarote and Fuerteventura 109

rabbits 15, 42–3, 96
radio 30–1
Raleigh, Sir Walter 53
religious services 31
reptiles 44, 82
restaurants 18–23, 24, 63, 87, 97, 105–6, 106, 116

riding 73
Río, El channel, approx 1 km wide, dividing Lanzarote from La Graciosa 41, 51, 80, 115, 116
Riscos de Famara 38, 75, 98, 114
roads 7
Romans 48, 49, 50
Roque del Este islet 84 m high, 1.2 km NE of Órzola 33, 112
rum 18
'Ruta de los Volcanes' 38, 66, 87, 88–9

sailing 74
Salinas de Janubio 58–9
Salinas del Río 59, 116
salt 44, 58–9, 92, 107
San Bartolomé (pop. 9151) sizeable village and municipal capital in central Lanzarote, 7 km N of Arrecife; dignified central square with church, *ayuntamiento* and municipal theatre (being refurbished in 1996) 18, 56
Santa, La small hamlet on W coast between the Timanfaya National Park and Playa de Famara, opposite the small round island of La Isleta. Nearby is the large complex of Club La Santa, dedicated to almost every form of sport 67, 75
self-catering 12
shopping 82–4, *83*
slavery 53
smoked salmon 15–16, 94–5, 104
Sóo rambling agricultural village near N coast but sheltered from north wind by an isolated group of hills; in other directions Sóo is surrounded by the wild and largely deserted plain of El Jable 57